Columbus's Industrial Communities: Olentangy, Milo-Grogan, Steelton

Tom Dunham

authorHOUSE®

AuthorHouse™
1663 Liberty Drive
Bloomington, IN 47403
www.authorhouse.com
Phone: 1-800-839-8640

First published by AuthorHouse 9/9/2010

ISBN: 978-1-4520-5970-9 (e)
ISBN: 978-1-4520-5969-3 (sc)

Library of Congress Control Number: 2010911936

Printed in the United States of America

This book is printed on acid-free paper.

Table of Contents

Prelude to Industrial Communities

Introduction

Columbus, Ohio did not begin its growth undergirded by manufacturing companies that were common in the early development of other Ohio cities, as Cincinnati, Cleveland, Akron, and Dayton. Historian Alfred Lee in 1892 wrote: "Columbus has the unique distinction of having been born a capital," [1] as opposed to an industrial beginning. Early on it appeared that industrial development held little interest to Columbus businessmen and investors. William Martin in his 1858 History of Franklin County wrote:

"Although Columbus always possessed a reasonable amount of wealth and money making talent, the attention of its capitalists never was until of late years much turned toward manufacturing, but more directed to speculating upon the production of others ... than to the creating new or additional wealth."[2]

After 1870, however, Columbus manufacturing began to sprout, yet this sector never dominated the local economy, as manufacturing employment throughout most of the city's history seldom exceeded twenty-five percent of the workforce. However, twenty-five percent of the economy was enough to give manufacturing a significant role in Columbus's growth and pattern of development.

While the Columbus's manufacturing was in its rapid growth stage from about 1870 to 1920, three clusters of manufacturing stood out. First identified in a 1921 neighborhood study of Columbus by Ohio State university sociologist, Roderick McKenzie,[3] who deliberately labeled these areas as "industrial communities" rather than industrial sites, for all three were characterized by adjoining neighborhoods of worker housing with companion retail that allowed easy walking from home to work and to shopping. As these communities were developing before and at the beginning of the 20th century Columbus was a walking city, as mass consumption of the private automobile had not yet intruded into the life of the average person, altering as it later would family and lifestyle patterns.

The first of McKenzie's factory clusters can be divided into two sections. The older section extended from Spruce Street (across from today's convention center) north to First Avenue, along the east bank of the Olentangy River. Separated by a railroad yard from the first section, the later developing section began near the downtown's edge at Spring Street and extended north along the Olentangy to Brodbelt Lane. Another cluster began development along the northbound tracks of the Cleveland, Columbus, Cincinnati, and St Louis Railroad. (Later this track became known as the Big Four tracks.) As this track extended from the Union Station at High and Naghten streets, the first factories located about one-half mile northeast of the depot, while others were built a short distance to the east and north near the intersection of

1

Fifth and Cleveland avenues. The third cluster was located partly outside and partly inside Columbus's south side boundary, near and around the intersection of Parsons Avenue and Marion Road. Common to all three clusters was their location adjacent to railroad networks, allowing convenient shipping of products and the receiving of supplies and raw material. Common also to all three factory clusters was the decision of the factory owners to locate at the outer fringe of the city, a location that would later be a disadvantage as Columbus grew around them.

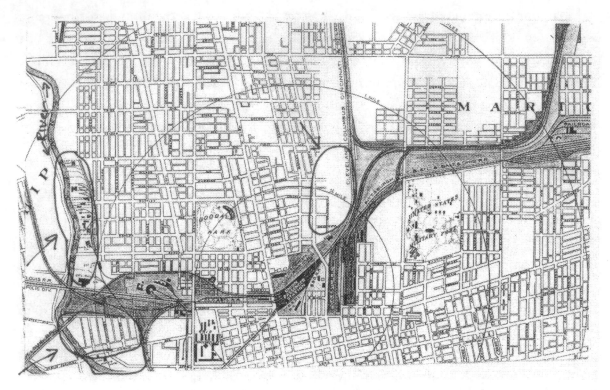

This 1893 map locates two of the three industrial clusters. The first is along the Olentangy River. Both sections are circled. The first section shows many factories, as indicated by the dark squares. The newer section, below and across the shaded railroad yard is not yet developed. The second cluster, also circled is north of the Union Station along the railroad tracks. The third cluster is well off the bottom of the map, about two to three miles south of the Union Station. (Columbus Metro Library)

Downtown Columbus

Before discussing the growth and decline of these industrial communities, a note on the downtown is in order, for Columbus's downtown, as was common in many 19th century American cities, became the site of the city's earliest industries.

Columbus's original 1812 plat designed as a grid with streets at right angles to one another extended several blocks to the east of the Scioto River, and to the north and south, the plat paralleled the river for about twelve blocks. About three blocks from the river and midway in the twelve-block length, the plat owners set aside a ten-acre square for a state capital building.

Aside from another donated ten acres for a state penitentiary, the plat owners would sell the lots, giving themselves a tidy profit. As the city grew, the downtown came to be considered as covering about four blocks to the north and south of the capital grounds, and from the Olentangy, the downtown extended to the capital grounds and about four blocks beyond it.

Since a river was a magnet for the siting of early industry, the Scioto all but guaranteed that Columbus's downtown would see its share of manufacturing, though by later standards, the downtown's early factories were small and for the most part without lasting influence.

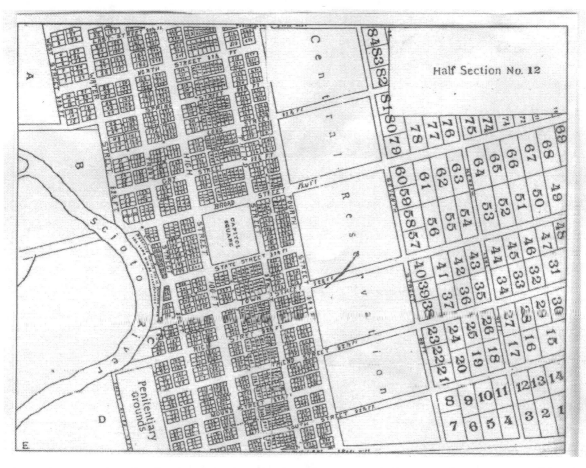

This is the 1812 plat of Columbus. The densely platted area around the Capital Square is roughly what most Columbus residents would consider today's downtown. Many early factories were built along the Scioto riverbank. Early 20th century commercial growth and the 1913 flood forced industry from the river area. (Columbus Metro Library)

Early manufacturing entrepreneurs saw two obvious advantages to a Scioto location within the plat. It not only would be a convenient source of water, but also in this environmentally innocent age, the river would also serve as a sewer for the disposal of factory waste, both free of charge. Two of the early riverbank factories included a saw mill built in 1819 near Rich Street (Rich is two blocks west of the capital grounds), and an 1826 cotton yarn plant between Rich and Friend (later Main) streets. Many such early businesses failed for want of a market and lack of transportation, but in a growing town, there is no lack of trying. By 1832, an enterpriser had built a steam-powered saw mill on the Scioto's eastern bank at Friend (Main) Street. During the 1840s, a paper mill operated on the bank of the river just north of Broad Street. Near the same riverbank location, the Columbus Woolen Factory began operations in 1851 and continued until 1870 when a fire destroyed the plant. In the 1850s, another steam-powered saw mill opened for nearly a decade near the edge of the downtown at Spring and Water streets. (Water Street extended along the river and was renamed Marconi Blvd in the late 1930s.)

A relatively successful business was the Franklin Foundry, which remained in operation from 1838 until 1857 at Town and Scioto streets. (Scioto Street, along the river, became Riverside Drive about 1931 and was renamed Civic Center Drive in the late 1940s.) One of the more successful early entrepreneurs was Joseph Ridgeway, who in 1832 established a foundry on the north side of Broad Street and the Scioto in order to manufacture plows. Going strong over two decades later, Ridgeway in 1848 began building steam engines, and in this period constructed a railroad car factory, manufacturing railroad rolling stock. Ridgeway died in the early 1850s, and Peter Hayden acquired the foundry. Hayden, having Ridgeway's business drive, established the Columbus Iron Works in 1857, producing pumps springs, and axles. The Hayden family would remain in business at the Broad and Scioto site for another half century.

The early shoe factories tended to locate a few blocks east of the Scioto, but very much in the downtown. By 1849 various shoe manufacturers employed about 200 workers, a few being women. The largest footwear factory, owned by A.C. Brown, employed about sixty. A long-lived shoe manufacturer was H.C. Godman (whom we will meet later in connection with Flytown), who opened a factory in 1865 on South High Street about two blocks south of the capital grounds. In 1923 the company moved about three blocks farther south to Fulton Street, and in 1953 still remained in operation with about 350 workers.

M.C. Lilly and Company was another downtown, but off-river company. Opening in the mid 1860s at Gay and Front streets, Lilly later erected a building on East Long Street, two blocks north of the capital grounds. Like Godman, Lilly was one of the few factories that would remain downtown over its life. Lilly, however, was not a smokestack factory, having a rather "clean" business producing regalia.

All of this downtown industry was dependent on efficient transportation for success. The Scioto and Olentangy rivers were helpful, and for some industries, they were essential, but they did not constitute a transportation network, the absence of which partly explains Columbus's late start in manufacturing development.

However, during the 1830s outside forces had already given a boost to many of the above businesses by bringing both a canal and an interstate road to Columbus. The Ohio and Erie Canal was a state enterprise that extended from Portsmouth at the southern end of the state to Lake Erie at the northern end. After seven years of construction, the canal opened for its entire north-south length in September 1832. However, the main route of the canal by-passed Columbus, as the surveyors about ten miles south of the city directed the route to the northeast around Columbus. To satisfy economic interests of the city the so-called Columbus feeder, a branch off the main canal was constructed from Lockbourne, Ohio extending north parallel to the Scioto River on its east side. About eleven miles in length, the feeder intersected with the Scioto in Columbus's downtown near Friend (Main) Street. After completion in September 1831, many businesses were established along the feeder, making effective use of the new state waterway.

Following soon after the canal the federally funded National Road entered Columbus as it made its way from Cumberland, Maryland to St. Louis. (Later it became Route 40 over its distance.) Entering Columbus on the east side, the road builders overlaid the new road on Friend Street, and upon reaching High Street, proceeded north for three blocks to Broad Street, then resumed a western direction across Ohio. At the Scioto River, the national crews paused in order to construct a new Broad Street bridge. However, Joseph Sullivant, son of Franklinton founder Lewis Sullivant, held bridge rights over the Ohio, allowing him to collect a toll from bridge users. Columbus residents contributed $8,000 to buy Sullivant's rights in order that a free national bridge could be constructed.

Together the canal and the National Road ended Columbus's relatively isolation from the rest of the state. National Road traffic, heavy in its early years, brought many travelers to Columbus, passing through to other points. Their purchases of supplies, wagon repairs, and shoeing of horses brought welcome commercial gains to Columbus merchants, as new businesses and small factories began to locate along the canal and the new federal road. With two transportation routes, one north-south and the other east-west, Columbus by the mid 1830s had become the crossroads of Ohio, the geography of which was instrumental in Columbus's population more than doubling from 2,435 in 1830 to 6,040 in 1840.

Factory growth in the downtown would continue for most of the 19th century. The Scioto riverbank, just three blocks from the capital grounds had become over the years cluttered with grimy, unsightly warehouses and workplaces, as a weak and caretaker city government did nothing to prevent such poor construction. It took a natural disaster to clear much of the downtown riverbank. Following the 1913 flood, Columbus voters in order to prevent a future flood approved in November 1916 a $3.5 million bond issue for the purpose of purchasing private property along the riverfront, allowing the river channel to be widened in front of the downtown. By 1920, the channel improvement was nearly complete.[4]

Although the flood forced many businesses from the downtown, a more fundamental reason had already been at work for about two decades making it imperative that industry move outward. The downtown in its early decades had been able to meet the acreage requirements of the city's small factories, but Columbus was growing. Its population in 1880, for example, was over 51,000 up from about 19,000 in 1860. Such expansion meant that industry had an increasing need for additional land, both for new factory sites, as well as expansion of existing factories. Yet the downtown in the closing decades of the 19th century had increasingly less land for industrial use.

Moreover, any land available in the downtown was becoming too expensive for factory use. Thus, industry toward the end of the 19th century was leaving the downtown, as commercial structures were becoming dominant. The most striking of the new buildings were the skyscrapers, made possible in the 1890s by the advent of steel framing and the perfection of the elevator, thereby making it possible to reduce land requirements by building upward rather than outward. Columbus's first skyscraper was the eleven-story, 1897 Wyandotte Building, designed by the noted Chicago architect of skyscrapers, Daniel Burnham. The Wyandotte is still in use today at the south side of Broad Street just west of High Street.

As factories departed and commercial construction grew in the 1890s, the early years of the 20th century saw the downtown turning into an architecturally central business district characterized by the dominant functions of retail, banking, insurance, lodging, and local and state government. Following closely after the Wyandotte opening, other steel-framed skyscrapers included the twelve-story 1900 Hayden Building at 16 E. Broad Street and the 1906 Capital Trust Building at 8 E. Broad, reaching sixteen-stories, both of which still stand and in use. In 1903, the twelve-story Harrison Building opened at 21 S. High Street, across from the Statehouse. Although still standing, the building is not recognizable as originally built, for in 1915 the Huntington Bank purchased it and in 1925 physically incorporated it into its new bank building. The Huntington's building with its dominant arch entrance still graces High Street, near the downtown's principal intersection with Broad. Another steel-framed skyscraper built in this period and still in use is the thirteen-story Atlas Building. Completed in 1905 with twelve-stories at the northeast corner of High and Long streets, it later was known as the Ohio Savings and Loan Trust Building.

Other significant structures that played a role in changing Columbus's downtown at the dawn of the 20th century included:

1) Chittenden Hotel – Opened in 1892 at High and Spring streets. It was rebuilt in 1895 after a fire andserved Columbus until it was razed in 1972.

2) Southern Hotel – Opened in 1897 at High and Main streets. It was renovated in 1985 and still serves travelers, though under the Westin name. In addition, the hotel maintains a theatre, a bar and restaurant for Columbus area residents.

3) Hartman Hotel – Opened in 1898 at Fourth and Main streets as a manufacturing building, but converted in 1901. Still in use, the Hartman was recently renovated for condo sales.

4) Virginia Hotel – Opened in 1908 as an apartment building, but converted to a hotel in 1911. It was closed and razed in 1961.

(Columbus's two primer hotels of the 20th century, the Deshler and the Neil House, were not a part of the early 20th century downtown skyline. The Deshler opened in 1916 at the northwest corner of Broad and High streets. It closed in 1968 and razed the following year. The third Neil House located on S. High Street across from the Statehouse was built in 1925 and razed in 1981.)

5) Lazarus, always Columbus's leading department store opened a new six-story emporium in 1909 at the northwest corner of High and Town streets, and from this location served Columbus's shoppers until 2004. Previous to 1909, Lazarus had operated for about a half-century at the southwest corner of High and town.

Although now new at the turn of the century, the government buildings should be noted, inasmuch as Columbus was both a state capital and a county seat. In 1887, the second Franklin County Courthouse had opened on High Street between Mound and Fulton streets, about three blocks south of the capital grounds. Characterized by a four-clock sided tower, this large, ornate building served the county until 1974 when it was demolished for a new courthouse. The 1872 Columbus City Hall was as the 20th century opened still in service to the city at 39 E. State Street (site of the present Ohio Theatre). In 1921 the old hall was destroyed by fire, leading to the 1926 construction of the present city hall at Broad and Front streets.

In the center of the downtown, the Statehouse had overlooked High Street since 1861 when it finally opened after a twenty-two year construction period. In 1901, the state constructed a Judiciary Building to the rear of the Statehouse on the Third Street side. When the Supreme Court moved out decades later, the legislature renamed the structure the Senate Building, and in another change, it was connected to the Statehouse as part of extensive renovations to the Capitol in the 1990s.[5]

As the downtown changed and grew in the early 1900s, the loss of the downtown factories as part of this change was not a series of events mourned by Columbus residents, for the industrial departure had come with a silver lining in the form of stately banks, attractive retail stores, opulent office towers, plush hotels, and in a few years motion picture theatres, all of which made the downtown a vibrant destination point for users and customers of the new venues.

However, as we will see, when the industrial communities lost their factories and employment sources about a half-century later, there was no silver lining replacing their losses. Instead, these communities experienced little but destruction, despair, and poverty.

This is an early 20th century view of Broad and High streets, the principal intersection of downtown. This photo connotes Columbus's growing central business district and the displacement of early factories. The view is north up High Street. The tallest building is the 1906 Capital Trust Building. It faces Broad Street, looking at the Statehouse. The building next to it is the 1900 Hayden Building. (Columbus Metro Library)

Railroad Impact

Although the need for more and cheaper land was a force pushing industry from the downtown, it was the railroad lines of the city that largely determined the new locations. As will be shown, the railroads were especially crucial to the early success and location of the factories within the industrial communities.

Columbus's railroad development began in 1851 with the completion of the Columbus and Xenia line connecting Columbus with Cincinnati. Additional rail lines were built through Columbus during the 1850s, and throughout the Civil War, continuing into the 1870s and 1880s. By 1890 fifteen separate railroads were using the city's train depots, the principal one being located on the east side of High Street near Naghten Street (the site of today's convention center). Although just north of the downtown, the Union Station can be considered a part of changing downtown as the 20th century approached. In the mid-1890s, High Street was raised over the many tracks entering the depot, and on the new viaduct, architect Daniel Burnham, the later designer of the Wyandotte Building, built a system of arched entrance facades, using Greek style columns, that would landmark this area of High Street for nearly eight decades.

In terms of industrial development, the most important rail line extended from Columbus to Athens in the mineral rich southeast part of Ohio. Columbus businessmen who raised stock subscriptions for funding the line initially called their firm the Mineral Railroad Company, but in 1867 the name became the Columbus and Hocking Valley Railroad Company, which completed the sixty-five mile line from Columbus to Athens in January 1871.Once the line opened there was little lag time getting resources to the railroad's freight yard on West Mound Street near the Columbus feeder. In the early 1870s, five coal mines had been operating in the southeastern counties, having a capacity of 250 carloads per day (though not that much was delivered each day). More mines soon opened, and by 1873 these coal fields were yielding 100 carloads per day for delivery to Columbus and beyond. One of the mines opening in the late 1870s contained iron ore.[6]

The opening of Ohio's southeast in the early 1870s changed the basis of Columbus's industry from one based on agriculture, as grain and sawmills, to one based on minerals. As outside economic interests began to realize the potential of Ohio's mineral resources, more industrialists began to locate in Columbus. Although not becoming a steel center, the newly mined coal and iron ore spawned the development of rolling mills, foundries, and machine shops in Columbus. As early as 1870, the Franklin Iron Company built a blast furnace in the city (a blast furnace will produce pig iron from iron ore). This development led booster optimism, leading an 1873 business prospectus to state: "The location of this furnace in our city will soon induce our own and foreign capitalists to invest in various other manufacturing enterprises... rolling mills, foundries furnaces, and pipe works, etc are springing up."[7]

Timber and natural gas from the southeast fields became the basis for other industries. Prior to the Civil War, Columbus had a small wagon and carriage industry. But timbering shipments from the southeast enabled many large and efficient factories to be built, turning Columbus into a national leader in carriage production. In addition, natural gas made the establishment of factories profitable. In 1886 the Columbia Natural Gas Company was organized to pipe natural gas to Columbus from Hocking, Perry, and Athens counties. The Columbus Board of Trade concluded in 1891 that the "striking of natural gas wells the past year within easy reach of the city has added an impetus to manufacturing pursuits ... natural gas is being used as fuel, both for domestic and manufacturing purposes."[8]

In the later part of the 19th century, the Board of Trade felt it had much to crow about regarding Columbus's manufacturing. In 1888,the Board reported that the city's manufacturing establishments totaled 915, having a payroll of about $6.3 million. The factories' workforce of over 14,000 manufactured products valued at over $26 million. Such statistics appear impressive, and a quarter century later, booster optimism must have been at high pitch, for by 1917 manufacturing product value had increased to over $100 million (for Columbus and Franklin County), the number of firms had grown to 1,321 with a workforce over 48,000.[9]

However, a more sober assessment of Columbus's manufacturing can be made by comparing the city's manufacturing with that of three other Ohio cities. The comparison is here made in the census years of 1980, 1910, and 1930.

1890

	# of mgf workers	**wages**	Product value	population
Columbus	13,421	6.8 million	22.9 million	88,150
Cincinnati	96,689	47.7 million	196.1 million	296,908
Cleveland	50,674	28.4 million	113.3 million	261,353
Dayton	12,047	5.9 million	22.4 million	61,620

1910

Columbus	16,428 workers	8.9 million	49.0 million	181,511 pop.
Cincinnati	60,192	31.1million	194.5 million	363,591
Cleveland	84,723	48.1 million	271.9 million	560,663
Dayton	21,549	12.5 million	60.4 million	116,577

1930

Columbus	32,340 workers	45.3 million	250.0 million	290,564 pop.
Cincinnati	114,068	157.6 million	933.3 million	451,160
Cleveland	176,840	276.2 million	1.5 billion	900,429
Dayton	42,591	64.8 million	330,3 million	200,982

Sources: 11th Census of United States, 1890, Manufactures, Part III
                13th Census of United States, 1910, Manufactures, Vol IX
                15th Census of United States, 1930, Manufactures, Vol III

The 1930 data, except for city population, reflects the industrial area rather than the physical city. For Columbus, the manufacturing data is for Franklin County. In absolute figures, the manufacturing dominance of Cincinnati and Cleveland is clear, but note that by 1910, the smaller city of Dayton was out producing Columbus in all manufacturing categories.

Yet Columbus's laggard manufacturing relative to other Ohio cities did not damage booster pride, for the city's economy has historically been diversified with finance, real estate, professional, and government as well as manufacturing playing a major role in local economic growth. Moreover, even within the manufacturing sector, Columbus's workforce has been diversified. McKenzie in his 1921 academic study of Columbus neighborhoods concluded that Columbus could not be classified as a city with a single dominant industry, as for example, Youngstown could with steel and Akron with rubber. Rather Columbus's was characterized by numerous small industries, each playing a significant manufacturing role.[10]

Part I

Olentangy and Flytown Industrial Community

Columbus's first industrial community, as mentioned previously, can be considered in two sections.

The earliest and the sector having nearby worker housing and retail, thereby making it in a physical sense, an industrial community extended along the east bank of the Olentangy River from Spruce Street north to First Avenue. Factory owners not only favored this area for the excellent rail connections (made clear by the map below) but also because the Olentangy, like the Scioto for the downtown factories, served as a water source and a convenient dump for factory waste. Soon after the Civil War, factories began to dot the banks of the Olentangy. The adjoining worker housing area, which grew along with the riverbank industry, provided an easy walk to the work sites, as the always cheaply built dwellings were located in a square directly east of the factories extending about four blocks to nearly Neil Avenue. This largely residential area as it became compact on small lots acquired the name "Flytown." As we will see shortly, there are at least two explanations for the name, neither of which would bring any renown to the area.

An 1865 Columbus map (not shown here) shows the future Flytown as nearly empty, devoid of even platting. Columbus annexed the Flytown area in 1871 as part of a larger area that extended north to the Ohio State University grounds. By 1878, the Flytown area, though not yet heavily populated, was fully platted over its generally accepted boundaries, which were: Buttles Avenue on the north, Spruce Street on the south, the factories in the west, and nearly to Neil Avenue on the east.

The map below shows the early Olentangy factories and Flytown in relation to notable markers: Goodale Park (G.P. on map), the Union Depot, and the Ohio Penitentiary (O.P.).

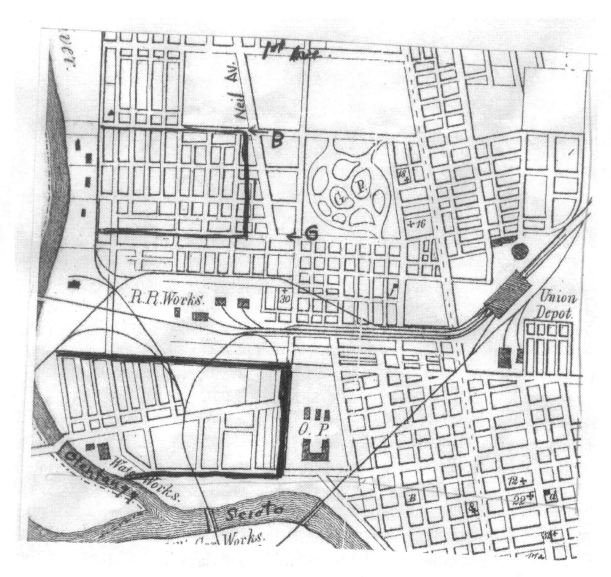

This 1878 map by Jacob Struder indicates that the Olentangy factories (black squares on map) began development in the 1870s. The worker housing area, later known as Flytown lay between Buttles Avenue (B in map) and Goodale Street (G on map) and enclosed by dark lines. The newer section of factories would develop south and across the railroad yard from the first – indicated by dark lines. (Columbus Metro Library)

The factories operating along the Olentangy by 1878, as partly dotted on the map were:

    Wassell Fire Clay Company
    Columbus Bent Works
    Axle and Skein Works
    H&R Smith Foundry
    Columbus Pipe Works

In addition, to the south of Goodale Street the Columbus Iron Company and the Columbus Rolling Mill were in operation. Throughout the 1870s the latter mill produced about 100 tons of rail stock per day. But the rails were iron, and by the late 1870s, railroads were increasingly ordering steel rails, a change that doomed the Columbus Rolling Works, as the mill was unable to convert from iron to steel production resulting in an 1884 closing. The failure of early manufacturing plants after just few years of operation was not uncommon, for many operations were controlled by one or a handful of owners having limited capital, and as business conditions changed, many lacked the investment necessary to alter production.

The Columbus Iron Works had better luck than its rolling mill neighbor, operating until the end of the century when it came under the control of Joseph Schonthal, who operated the factory into the 1930s. Most of the early Olentangy factories – Columbus Bent Works, Axle & Skein, the Smith foundry, and Columbus Pipe Works did not survive the 1870s. The Wassell Fire Clay Company lasted a decade longer, closing operations in the late 1880s.

Factories – 1890s

As rail lines increased and Flytown population grew, new factories opened along the Olentangy replacing the 1870s plants that had closed. For some ceasing operations meant only that the factory was reorganized under new ownership. For example, the Columbus Pipe Works of the 1870s evolved into the Ohio Pipe Works, and by the 1890s the same works had expanded and become the United States Cast Iron Pipe and Foundry Company, which was a Flytown employment source until nearly 1930. A section of a 1910 map below shows the many factories that had opened along the riverbank over the past twenty years.

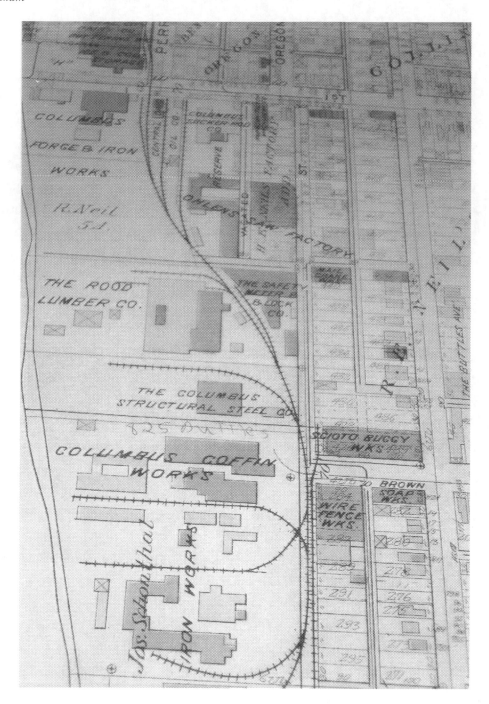

1) At the top of the map to the north of First Street is the Capital City Dairy Company. This butter and margarine producing company moved to this location from downtown on E. Third Street about 1900. In the mid 1920s, the company became the Capital City Products Company and had added vegetable oils, cheese and horseradish to its product line. It would become the Olentangy's oldest surviving company.

2) Columbus Forge and Iron Company began operations at the foot of First Street in the late 1890s. A successful company, Columbus Forge survived until the mid 1950s.

3) Rood Lumber Company opened just south of Columbus Forge in the 1890s building crates and boxes until ceasing operations in the mid 1920s.

4) Columbus Structural Steel Company opened about 1909 next to Rood Lumber. The company manufactured ornamental iron products, rivets, bolts, reinforced rods, and other building materials until the mid 1920s.

5) Columbus Coffin Company began making burial caskets in 1898 at the end of Buttles Avenue. A successful company for over a half-century until the mid 1950s when an urban renewal project made its Olentangy location untenable.

Other companies from First to Buttles streets in 1910 as shown on the map include an ice company, Ohlen's Saw Factory, Central Ohio Oil Company, Safety Meter and Lock Company, and the Mail Crane Works. The oil company had moved from the downtown on South High Street about 1908 to locate at the foot of First Street next to a railroad line, remaining there until the late 1940s when under the name of Sinclair Refining Company moved to north Columbus. In addition to the factories along the Olentangy, the Weiland Pump Factory had in 1910 relocated from downtown to Spruce Street, several blocks east of the river, which placed it within Flytown's boundaries. Weiland would operate at Spruce Street for over a half-century, making it one of the areas longest surviving companies.

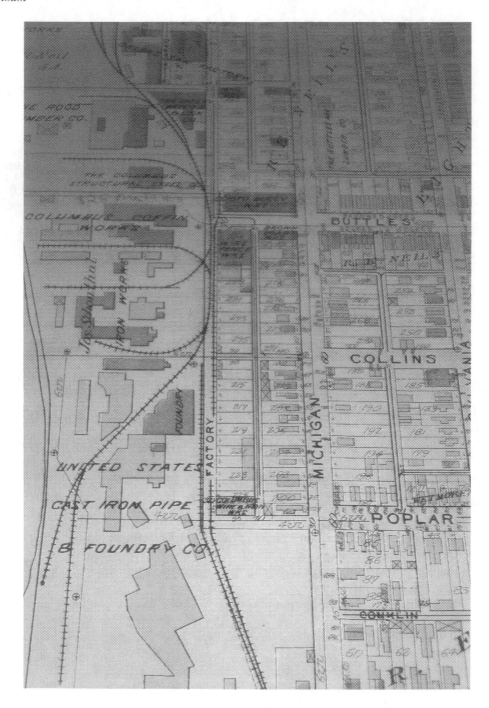

The above section of the same 1910 map shown previously continues with the Olentangy factories from Buttles south to Goodale Street. A large factory here is the Joseph Schonthal Iron Works, also having plant buildings to the south of Goodale, and as previously mentioned would survive into the 1930s. The United States Cast Iron Pipe and Foundry, consumed an entire block near Goodale, and would operate until about 1930. Other 1910 factories in this area Brown Soap Works, Wire Fence Works, Scioto Buggy Works, and the Columbus Wire and Iron Works. Some of these plants were located on Factory Street among private housing, something not uncommon in Flytown, which never experienced single use zoning that separated residential from industrial use.[11]

To Flytown's east and north lay the Neil Avenue residential district, an upscale development that began about 1890. When most of the housing was completed about 1910, the district extended from Goodale Street north about eight blocks to Fifth Avenue. Some of Columbus's most wealthy and influential families built architecturally designed homes in this district, many with five and six bedrooms, dance ballrooms, and carriage houses. Nearly all were brick of Queen Anne and other Victorian design, many with turrets, conical towers, and large porches. This housing along Neil Avenue and the cross streets is nearly all intact today, and forms part of the Victorian Village, established in 1973. Because the Neil Avenue housing was so affluent in comparison with that of Flytown, the eastern boundary of Flytown would stop short of Neil Avenue and would not cross Buttles Avenue to the north.[12]

Second Olentangy Factory Section

To Flytown's south, that is, across Spruce Street lay the railroad yards, and next to these yards lay a chunk of land that extended to the edge of the downtown at Spring Street. Although this later section of factories generated wealth, the downside was filth and grime. Writing in 1976, the Columbus Chapter of the American Institute of Architects called this area "…a no man's land of factories, warehouses, parking lots, and railroads. The area sees a good deal of vehicular traffic but few pedestrians…"[13] This characterization changed little since 1910, for a city map of that year shows it as a factory and warehouse area interspersed with narrow, dead end streets and a spider like web of railroad tracks with spur lines leading to factory shipping doors. The eastern boundary of this area was the 1833 Ohio Penitentiary, monstrosity with a twenty-four foot high wall that extended along Dennison Avenue from the railroad yard all the way to Spring Street. Dublin Avenue, was the principal street through the factory section, extending from the penitentiary at Dennison west to the river, and bridging the Olentangy.

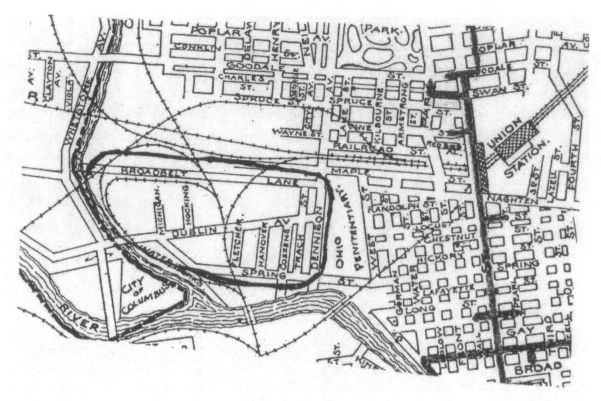

This cut out from a 1911 Columbus map illustrates the street pattern that developed within the newer cluster if Olentangy factories. The section is directly to the left of the penitentiary. Note the rail lines through the area. Not shown are the numerous spur tracks to the factories. (To the immediate right of the penitentiary is the location of today's Nationwide Arena and to the prison's left at Dublin and Dennison, now Neil Ave, is the site of the 2009 baseball stadium.) (Columbus Metro Library)

Development of this second section of factories did not begin until just after 1900. An 1890 city map indicates that the municipal water plant was the sole structure between the prison and the river. By 1903 the Columbus Buggy Company had relocated along Dublin Avenue from its initial location on the southwest corner of High and Naghten streets (where Nationwide Insurance is today). While at its High Street plant for quarter-century, Columbus Buggy had become one of Columbus's larger industries, as about 1,200 workers in the early 1890s manufactured about 100 carriages per day. Annual sales in this period to both a national and international market reached two million dollars. But the nationwide depression of the mid 1890s proved the beginning of the end for Columbus Buggy. The hammer blow to the carriage industry came a few years into the new century when the private automobile became mass produced. However, Columbus Buggy struggled on, moving to Dublin Avenue where it began the production of an electric car, called the Columbus Electric. This effort failed, as the industry was unable to produce a long lasting battery. A switch to the manufacture of a gasoline driven automobile also failed, for Columbus Buggy was unable to compete with Henry Ford and Detroit. Columbus Buggy finally folded in the aftermath of the 1913 flood.[14]

Having a much longer life in the area was the Union Fork and Hoe Company, which began operations in Columbus in 1860, and moved in 1907 along Dublin Avenue beside Columbus Buggy. Benefiting from the efficient railroad connections for shipment of its manufactured tools and other implements, Union Fork remained in operation at this site until the mid 1990s

The largest company in the industrial area between the penitentiary and the Olentangy was the Jaeger Machine Company. Like Columbus Buggy and Union Fork and Hoe, Jaeger began operations elsewhere in Columbus and relocated to Dublin Avenue. Jaeger initially incorporated in 1906 while on the west bank of the Scioto along Rich Street. Although high enough on the riverbank to escape the waters of the 1913 flood, projects for flood control forced Jaeger to move operations across the river where the company acquired about twenty acres along Dublin Avenue next to Union Fork. Driven to an early success by sales of its patented cement mixer, Jaeger prospered with a continuing flow of new construction equipment – pumps, winches, air compressors, and road paving machinery. Its successful products, marketed nationally and internationally enabled Jaeger to survive on Dublin Avenue until 1992 when it closed.[15]

Although Columbus Buggy failed in its effort to become a car company, the failure did not deter a second attempt from the same location. In 1919 the Allen Motor Car Company moved from Fostoria, Ohio and took over part of the old Columbus Buggy building. Allen attempted to find a niche in the automobile market by producing touring cars. But by the early 1920s, small companies stood little chance to successfully compete with the giants in Detroit, and Allen gave up the effort in 1929.

These three or four companies were merely the largest plants in this Olentangy cluster. Crammed along Dublin Avenue were some ten additional factories, warehouses, and other businesses. By 1925, there were, for example, two coal yards, a storage company, a lumber company, a box company, and a casket company. Moreover, within a single building, a security company, a lighting company, and an equipment company did business.

This area was not much of a place for residential dwellings, but early in the century, houses nevertheless were built, and for 1925, the city directory lists seventeen dwellings along Dublin Avenue across from Jaeger and Union Fork and Hoe. After the 1920s, the number dwindled, and by 1950, residents had abandoned the area.

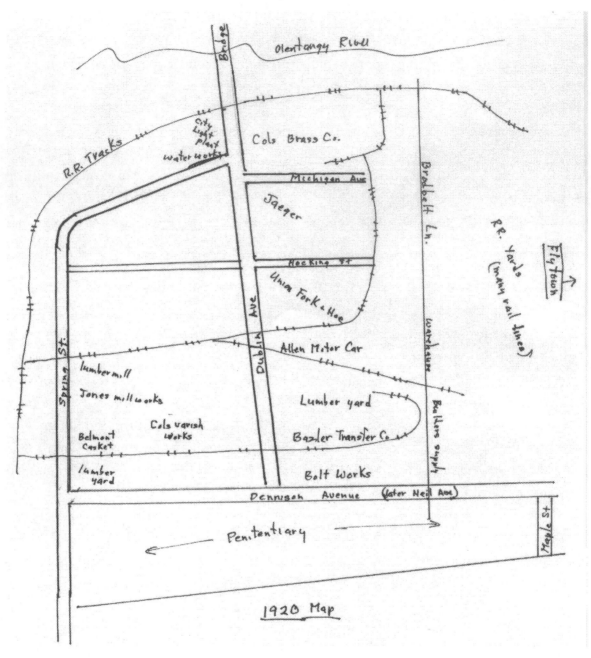

This hand drawing from a 1920 Columbus real estate map illustrates the chaotic appearance and seemingly disorganized layout of the newer section of the Olentangy factory cluster. Nearly everything in this area was eventually demolished, Jaeger and Union Fork lasting until about the mid 1990s. Allen Motor Car was the site of the earlier Columbus Buggy Factory, now the location of the Buggy Works, a condo development.

Flytown Housing

With the advent of factories along the Olentangy, the federal government designated the area a point of entry for arriving immigrants. This designation and employer recruitment in this labor intensive age drove the increase in Flytown's population. The newcomers came largely without funds, without meaningful assets, and without job skills, but Flytown offered cheap housing and unskilled jobs in the neighboring factories. With heavy immigration, small, inexpensive houses were built so fast, they seemed, as some observers said, to "fly up overnight." Thus began one of the undocumented sources of name "Flytown." A less charitable origin of the name was provided by Ohio State University researcher, McKenzie, who wrote in his 1921 study: Flytown received "this name on account of the migrating tendencies of workers employed in nearby factories, also on account of the lawlessness of the place."[16]

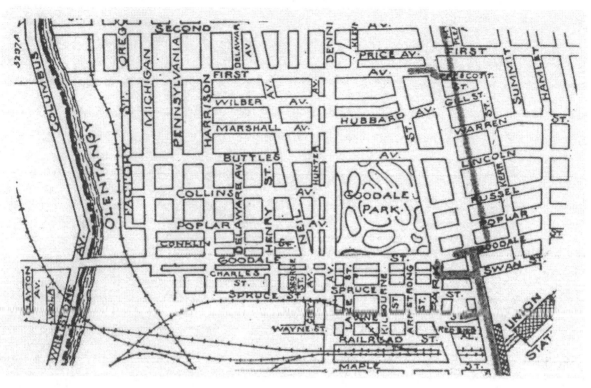

This section of a 1911 Columbus map shows the Flytown worker housing area. Although the factories extended to First Street, the Flytown housing ended on the north side at Buttles Avenue. To the north of Bulttles was higher housing quality, the area near Neil Avenue being part of today's Victorian Village. (Columbus Metro Library)

In the 1890s and 1900s, many Italians immigrated to Flytown, finding unskilled factory work in the nearby work sites. But a significant number did not head for the iron works or the buggy factory, choosing instead to become commercial entrepreneurs. A study of Italians in Flytown by Francesca Colonna Helton[17] found that in 1896 there were two Italian owned saloons in the 400 block of W. Goodale Street, and by 1906 two additional Italians had opened saloons on the same street within a block of the first two. In 1916, she reported that Italians owned three barber shops, four groceries, and three shoe stores – all on W. Goodale. In the next decade to 1926, Helton's study found the following additional Italian businesses had opened:

- Several groceries located on Goodale, Henry, and Harrison streets.
- Two shoe repair shops on Goodale Street.
- A tailor at 329 W. Goodale Street.
- A lunch room at 414 W. Goodale Street.

From the beginning, W. Goodale became Flytown's principal commercial and retail street. In addition to the Italian owned businesses, the street was home to many other immigrant and native American owned shops. In 1927, an incomplete sample of Goodale Street businesses showed a Greek restaurant, two pharmacies, three dry goods stores, two barbers, four confectioneries, a cigar shop, three billiard halls, a physician, and a dentist. At the end of Goodale near the river, a paper stock company and a tire and rubber company operated.

Although Goodale was Flytown's shopping and business venue, it was never an exclusive business street, as many Flytown residents lived among the retail shops, making W. Goodale a popular and lively gathering place. Of Goodale Street, a 1902 report stated that Flytown's principal street flourished with "shops of butchers and grocers, barber establishments, dingy and glorious saloons, all crowded between uninviting dwellings more or less adorned by board and lodging signs."[18] Until prohibition beginning in 1919, saloons were social hangouts for men of all ages where they played cards and dart games along with enjoying a glass of beer. Flytown enjoyed two social institutions that added a measure of stability to the neighborhood, one being the St Francis of Assisi Church. Completed in 1896 by the Italians at the corner of Buttles and Harrison streets, it was called by Francesca Helton and offshoot of the Sacred Heart Church a few blocks east in today's Italian Village. St Francis remains today a well-maintained structure and still serving area Catholics.

The second institution was the Godman Guild, a settlement house having its origin in the 1890s, when a group of middle-class reformers headed by Anna Keagle, upset by the prevalence of drunkenness and drab home life, formed the First Neighborhood Guild, which became a settlement house of the type pioneered by Jane Addams in Chicago. In 1899, Henry Godman, a wealthy Columbus shoe manufacturer, became impressed with the reformers' work and contributed $10,000 to start a fund drive that resulted in the construction of a three-story, twenty-room house at 468 W. Goodale Street. Opening in November 1900, the new settlement house had two kindergarten classrooms, reading and smoking rooms, a public bath, and classrooms for domestic science. Soon classes were being held for cooking, sewing, and woodworking. The third floor was reserved as living quarters for the staff. In honor its principal benefactor, the house was named the Godman Guild House.[19] The Godman Guild would serve Flytown's residents throughout the neighborhood's history, for the area remained poor and in some ways dysfunctional. Thus, the mission of a settlement house would continue.

During the World War I period and into the early 1920s, Flytown began to change. The hard working immigrants of the early 1900s were becoming assimilated and working their way to better areas of the city. The Italians, for example, had increasingly moved to east of High Street (later known as Italian Village), to the Hilltop on the west side, to the independent village of Grandview Heights, and to San Margarita to the northwest part of Columbus. A historical plaque erected by the Franklin County Historical Society in 1961 and now located in the southwest section of Goodale Park called Flytown's once seventeen nationalities "democracy's melting pot for the city of Columbus." This statement had become outdated by the early 1920s.

As the immigrants departed for other Columbus neighborhoods, Flytown became more overcrowded and remained poor, as large numbers of both whites and blacks from southern states took up residence in the cheap housing. Arriving for war work in the factories, these two groups remained and dominated Flytown's population during the 1930s, 1940s, and until the neighborhood came to an end during the late 1950s. According to McKenzie's study, as early as 1921, the residents of West.Goodale Street were nearly all black, and by 1950 nearly forty-seven percent of Flytown's housing units were occupied by blacks. These groups lacked the upward mobility of the earlier immigrants, thereby hindering the prospect of economic improvement. McKenzie, in his 1921 Columbus study called attention to the immigrants relatively faster move upward. He wrote: "This is especially true with respect to immigrant neighborhoods. The economic progress of the immigrant is faster, as a rule, than that of the slum dwelling American. Consequently more immigrants than Americans graduate from the poorer neighborhoods."[20] For the blacks, upward mobility was especially difficult, as Columbus housing discrimination forced them to stay put.

Following the population shift from immigration diversity to the dominance of southern whites and blacks, Flytown in the words of a Victorian Village newsletter article "began a slow but steady journey into economic and cultural despair."[21]

As Flytown was socially deteriorating, the area workplaces along the Olentangy, nevertheless, remained largely viable even through the depression of the 1930s. In 1937, for example, the area along the riverbank from First Avenue to Buttles remained filled with operating factories. These were:

- Columbus Forge and Iron.
- Carbo Oxygen
- International Derrick
- Columbus Coffin Company
- Sinclair Oil
- Ohlen Bishop Saws
- Ohio State Stove and Manufacturing Company

From Buttles Avenue south to Goodale, there were ten more companies, including the very large Joseph Schonthal Iron and Steel Company (this company would not survive to 1940). Other companies in the area were Scott Vineer, Cherry Burrell, E.M. Hulse, and on

Michigan Avenue, one block east of the riverbank, Hazlett Furnace, International Stacy, and Commercial Paste operated. In 1921 the Dresser-Ideco Company opened a factory on Michigan Avenue in order to manufacture structural steel products, such as derrick equipment and products for the aircraft industry. As late as 1953, Dresser employed 400 workers at this site.[22]

However, the persistence of the Olentangy factories did little to change the opinion of Flytown among Columbus residents as they observed the area from the outside. To many, Flytown " was synonymous with factory filth and foreigners." Another epithet applied to the neighborhood was "a grimy industrial district." In her 1980 history of Columbus, Betty Garrett called Flytown in the 1920s "the worst slum in the city."

This unidentified street in Flytown, labeled only as a " Typical street in Goodale slum area." (Columbus Metro Library)

A 1930 study by the Godman Guild concluded that "Flytown was the poorest and most unsatisfactory housing district of Columbus." Before World War I, Flytown had many pockets of housing deterioration that continued to get worse during the 1920s leading to a 1933 federal housing survey that found "extensive dilapidation." Poor housing is generally associated with overcrowding, and so it was in Flytown. By the early 1920s, the housing lots were all built over, and no new housing was built during the balance of the 1920s and none in the 1930s. As in-migration of southern whites and blacks continued, Flytown's housing capacity was stretched beyond the limit. The Columbus Call and Post newspaper reported that in the 1940s doubling up had become common. The paper wrote: "Many homeowners had renters comprising whole families who shared the kitchen and bathroom equality." Housing deterioration was therefore the result. [23]

Housing continued its downward spiral. The 1950 federal census found that fifty-two percent of Flytown's dwelling units had no private bath or were otherwise dilapidated, and twenty-five percent had no running water. Of some 1,300 dwellings, seventy-five percent were rented. At the beginning of Flytown's razing in 1957, the Columbus City Plan concluded that housing along the western end of Goodale Street was fifty to ninety percent substandard. A Columbus Dispatch reporter wrote in 1980 that between 1924 and 1952, Flytown's property values had fallen forty-one percent. Columbus historian Ed Lentz summarized Flytown this way:

> Flytown was not a pretty place for most of its history, Its main streets were full of saloons and vice dens that ran all night and tried their best to separate poor people from what little money they had. But the housing in Flytown was cheap and people were not particular about their neighbors. For hundreds of immigrants it was simply the only place they could find, at first.[24]

Flytown Razed

Such substandard housing made Flytown in the eyes of Columbus authorities a slum. In the immediate post World War II period, there were many Flytowns in cities across the country, leading to the passage of the Federal Housing Act of 1949. The urban renewal section of this act gave Columbus authorities the chance to destroy Flytown and rebuild the physical area. Under the urban renewal program, the federal government would fund two-thirds of the cost of purchasing slum housing and razing it. The cleared area would then be sold below market to private developers who under a local plan would redevelop the area.

The vehicle for the destruction and redevelop would be the Columbus Urban Renewal Authority or CURA, a local government agency required to be created by the federal act and having the power of eminent domain. From its creation in 1952, CURA was manned and controlled by Columbus bankers, builders, and other business leaders. Other than to protest CURA decisions, neither the Godman Guild, the social service agency for Flytown, nor the residents of Flytown, played a role in the neighborhood's economic fate. By 1953 CURA officially determined that Flytown would be razed, and the cleared area would be rebuilt with middle class apartments with an adjoining commercial strip. After Columbus voters passed a 1956 bond issue for the funding of the city's one-third share of the cost, CURA spent the next three years, condemning, purchasing, and bulldozing Flytown's housing, businesses, and other structures, leaving the residents to find other housing, though there were federal funds for relocation costs.

Relocation costs were not, however, available to business owners. If a business owner also owned the storefront, he was of course paid for the real estate, but received nothing for the lost business, a policy that meant business owners who did not own their storefront were left with an empty bag. In 1950, just three years before the urban renewal plan finalized the commercial destruction, the Columbus city directory listed forty-one businesses along W. Goodale Street.

Many of the proprietors tried to persuade CURA to renovate their storefronts rather than bulldoze them, but CURA was unbending in its plan to raze all of Flytown.[25]

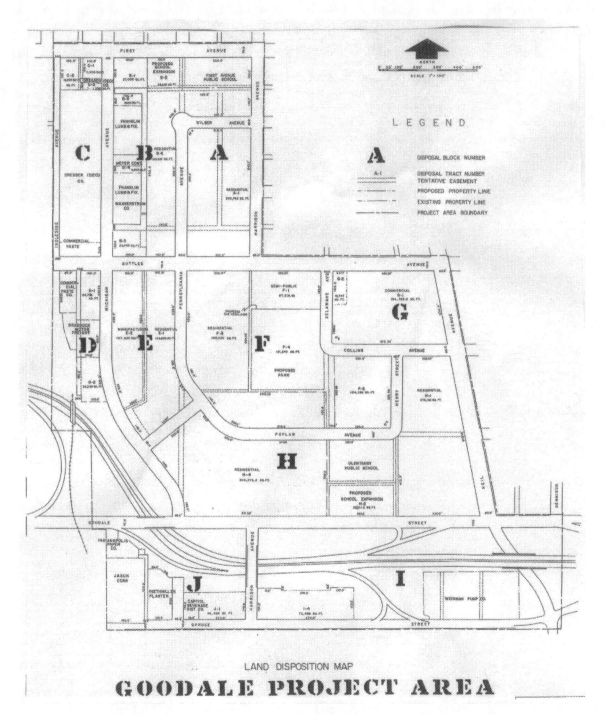

LAND DISPOSITION MAP

GOODALE PROJECT AREA

This is the plan of the Columbus Urban Renewal Commission for the reconstruction of the cleared area of the former Flytown. Between Buttles and Goodale was the housing area. Note that the internal streets were torn up and a new street pattern laid out. Sections J and I at the bottom show the future I-670. As it curved upward or north to bridge the Olentangy River, the highway builders had taken a large section of the factory sites. Sections A and B, north of Buttles was not a part of Flytown. This area is known as Harrison West. Section G is the site of the current shopping strip and parking lot. (Columbus Metro Library)

In May 1961, the City of Columbus signed a contract with United Redevelopment Corporation to redevelop forty-seven acres as outlined in the above map. By February 1968, the $15 million project, housing over 2,000 was complete, and Columbus officially closed out the Flytown urban renewal project. The new area or neighborhood would be known as "Thurber Village," in memory of Columbus writer, James Thurber, who made a name for himself on the staff of New Yorker magazine. Thurber's career was devoid of any involvement in urban planning, real estate, or urban renewal, but his name gave the project a benign feel, which is what Columbus authorities wanted. "Flytown II" would never do.

Although the Thurber Apartments (there were different names for other apartment buildings) appear to be satisfactory middle class dwellings for individuals and couples, holding largely white collar jobs, these structures are testament to the widely held view that federal urban renewal projects were not known for architectural distinction. Moreover, the designers and planners made no attempt to design the many apartment buildings to be compatible in style with the homes of the neighboring Victorian Village. Deliberately so Thurber Village clashed with Victorian Village.

The planners did, however, leave an area for a pleasant, rolling hill park near the center of the village, called Wheeler Park, a part of which in 2009 was set aside for a popular dog park. Perhaps the most unsatisfactory part of the new village is the Thurber Village Shopping Center, occupying a very visible square block beginning at Neil and Buttles avenues. The shopping consists of a linear strip of retail stores set back a block off Neil Avenue. An unsightly surface parking lot stretches from the store fronts to Neil. In order to obtain the needed space for the parking lot, CURA included seven Neil Avenue houses between Buttles and Collins avenues as part of the area to be razed. The Victorian Village newsletter later took note of this commonplace 1950s design, the author writing: "A large surface parking lot fronting Neil Avenue cuts a massive scar into what would otherwise an unbroken urban boulevard."

The parking lot formerly contained houses of the Neil Avenue Residential Area. The urban renewal commission condemned and razed seven homes in the block from Buttles to Collins avenues for the shopping strip parking lot. This is the "massive scar" in the street criticized by the Victorian Village newsletter.

The factory cluster dating from the 1870s along the riverbank was outside the urban renewal area, and the factories were not required to move. However, as the plan design above shows, the interbelt expressway, later known as I-670, was in the planning stage in the 1950s, and at the time an exit ramp was designed to run through a major portion of the riverfront factory sites. This became a reality a few years later, and thus nearly an entire block of the old factory sites from Goodale to Buttles was destroyed.

By 1958, the old factories along the riverbank were nearly all gone. On Michigan Avenue, one block from the riverbank, light factories continued to exist, notably Dresser-Ideco, still fabricating steel. In the Michigan and Buttles street area Commercial Paste, Motor Kool Products Company, and a junkyard continued in operation. Ten years later, they had all left, and the residents of Thurber Village had largely clean, non-polluting office buildings as neighbors along Michigan Avenue. The last surviving riverbank factory was the Capital City Dairy Company, located just south of First Avenue, and thus the farthest of the older factories from the bulldozers. As it increased its product line, the company became the Industrial Products Group in 1982, and lasted nearly another two decades, closing in the spring of 2001, displacing 112 employees. By then, the old dairy company was known as the A.C Humko plant, owned by a Tennessee Company.[26]

Olentangy Second Section Cleared

As barely a trace of the first section of the industrial community consisting of the Olentangy factories and Flytown remain, so the second section from the railroad yards to Spring Street has just as effectively been obliterated. However, the factories and businesses of the later section were not subject to a forced removal, as was the case in Flytown. Not being part of an urban renewal project, the factories between the penitentiary and the Olentangy were allowed to die a natural death before a move was made to redevelop the area

When a federal judge ordered the penitentiary closed in 1984 (but not razed), Columbus planners could now perceive a large canvas on which to formulate design plans, a canvas that would stretch from the High Street and Naghten area west past the penitentiary site, across Dennison (now Neil Avenue), past the sites of Columbus Buggy, Union Fork, and Jaeger, and to the Olentangy. First, however, we consider the area on the east side of the penitentiary to High Street. For decades this area had been a grimy warehouse district, undergoing deterioration since World War II, thereby allowing Columbus authorities to consider its clearing. But the prison was the bone in the throat, and it first had to be razed prior to serious planning. Yet even before the prison closing, Nationwide Insurance Company took the initial move in the renovation of this area by completing in 1976 a forty-story office tower set in a well-landscaped surrounding area. Built on the southwest corner of High and Naghten Streets, the new tower occupied the site of Columbus Buggy before its 1902 move to the west side of the penitentiary. Catty-cornered to Nationwide, the Hyatt Regency Hotel and the Ohio Center opened in 1979 at the site of the former Union Station that had been demolished in 1977. After Nationwide built two more towers in the 1980s adjacent to its first, the city of Columbus complemented the Hyatt and the Ohio Center in 1993 by completing a new Greater Columbus Convention Center just north of the Hyatt extending to Goodale Street.

But all of this High Street construction was on the edge of the deteriorating warehouse area, and little could be done in the inner part while the penitentiary stood. Finally, the old prison was demolished in 1996. In the old factory area, Jaeger as we have seen closed operations in 1992 and abandoned the site followed about two years later by the departure of Union Fork and Hoe. With the buggy factory and Allen automobile works long gone, over seventy-five acres west of the former penitentiary could be planned for development.

The section to the east was somewhat smaller, but it became the heart of the soon to be Arena District Located between Park Street (a block west of High) and Neil Avenue, the centerpiece of the district would be the hockey arena, but construction was delayed after voters rejected two attempts to increase the sales tax that would fund the arena. Nationwide Insurance Company then agreed to put together a privately financed package that resulted in the completion of the Nationwide Arena in fall 2000, and in the same year the Columbus Blue Jackets of the National Hockey League played their first game in the new arena. The rest of the district's amenities – restaurants, taverns, office buildings, movie theatre, and apartments and condominiums sprouted rapidly. Respected financial institutions, as Fifth Third Bank and Charles Schwab saw fit to locate in the district. A linear park, fronted by an arch from the old Union Station, extended from Nationwide Blvd (formerly Naghten Street) south to meet the riverfront park along the Scioto.

This is a contemporary view of the plaza in front of the hockey arena, the centerpiece of the Arena District. Restaurants, taverns, apartments, and businesses surround this former deteriorating warehouse area.

The old factory section between Neil Avenue (formerly Dennison) and the Olentangy was slower to join the vibrant upper part of the district. To this day, the former Jaeger site near the river still lay vacant. But in 2002, architects and builders retained many of the brick walls of the Columbus Buggy Company and constructed condominium units called the Buggy Works. Facing Neil Avenue and alongside the old factory road, the still labeled Dublin Avenue, the Columbus Clippers minor league baseball team acquired a new stadium, opening in spring 2009.[27]

Over all, city planners are no doubt proud of their creation, for it is fair to say that the Arena District works superbly. It is lively, vibrant, busy, and attractive – a Columbus destination point. With the district well intact, the obliteration of both sections of the

Olentangy Industrial Community became nearly total. In the former Flytown, only St. Francis of Assisi Church has survived. In the second section, it is difficult to find anything left other than the walls of the buggy factory and the deteriorating Municipal Light Plant still facing the site of the former Jaeger plant.

The saga of the Olentangy Industrial Community may be summed up by paraphrasing the macho military cliché: "It became necessary to save the community by destroying the community."

Part II

Milo-Grogan Industrial Community

A network of railroad tracks extending northeast from Columbus's Union Station at High and Naghten streets led to the formation of second manufacturing cluster of factories. Beginning about 1870 a set of tracks that would later form a square began to take shape, as less than a mile from the railroad depot, a rail line divided into a northbound and a eastbound direction, thereby forming the left side and the bottom of a square. By the mid 1880s, track extensions had made the railroad square a reality. Within this square, the communities of Milo and Grogan would begin their development in the late 1880s. (More on these communities later).

But before the railroad square was inclosed, some industrial entrepreneurs, satisfied with a single rail line, began to locate along the northbound track that initially belonged to the Cleveland, Columbus, Cincinnati, and St. Louis Railroad. In 1870 Kilbourne and Jacobs, an early manufacturer of wheelbarrows for farmers, opened a plant just one-half mile northeast of the Union Station. The factory, located on the west side of the track, fronted Lincoln Street, a narrow street three blocks south of First Avenue. Kilbourne became one of Columbus's most successful early manufacturing companies. A few years after opening Kilbourne developed a line of hand trucks, selling about forty percent of this product to the New York Central Railroad. In 1890 the Ohio State Journal, a Columbus newspaper, reported that with 400 to 600 workers, the company was producing about 150,000 hand trucks annually, giving Kilbourne nearly one million dollars in annual sales.[1]

A decade after Kilbourne opened, the Berry Brothers Bolt Company began operations just to the north of Kilbourne along the same railroad line, facing First Avenue. A few years after its founding, Berry Brothers constructed a new factory building in 1888, which is now on Columbus's register of historic buildings, and currently remains in use by other businesses. Although Berry Brothers would survive until 1997, it was never a large company, as employment rarely exceeded seventy workers.

Following Kilbourne and Berry Brothers along the northbound railroad line, the Jeffrey Manufacturing Company built an industrial plant that would soon dwarf its two predecessors. Jeffrey like many Columbus companies got its start in or the near the downtown, in Jeffrey's case on the west bank of the Scioto across the river from downtown. While on the riverbank, the company was called the Lechner Mining Machine Company, after Francis Lechner who had invented a chain-driven, air-powered machine that would cut coal from an underground seam. This machine obviously was a productivity boon to coal companies, who formerly employed miners to lie on their sides swinging an axe at the exposed coal. Joseph Andrews Jeffrey had been a majority shareholder in the Lechner company from its 1877 incorporation.

During its first decade, business grew steadily, and Jeffrey seeing the potential of mining equipment, resigned his position as cashier at Columbus's Commercial Bank, and bought out Lechner and other minority shareholders. He then changed the firm's name to "Jeffrey Manufacturing Company," and in 1888 purchased four acres along the northbound rail line, across First Avenue from Berry Brothers. By the late 1940s, the four-acre site had grown to forty-eight acres containing some forty buildings stretching from south of First Avenue to the north of Second Avenue, and from the railroad tracks to Fourth Street.

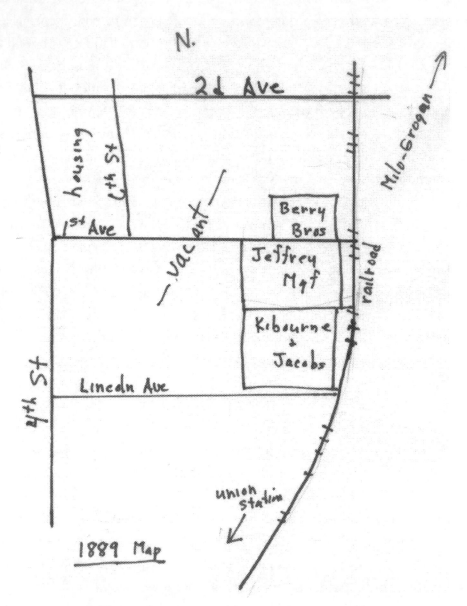

This drawing was copied from an 1889 Columbus map. It shows three early companies along the northbound railroad tracks that extended from the Union Station, all are from a half-mile to a mile from the depot. First to locate here was Kilbourne in 1870, followed by Berry Brothers in 1880, and Jeffrey in 1888. Later Jeffrey would swallow Kilbourne and build plants over all the area from First Avenue to Lincoln and move north, taking nearly all the land to Second Avenue over to Fourth Street. Berry Brothers would not expand, but would remain a fixture at this site for another century.

As J.A. Jeffrey took over the helm, the company's coal cutting machine driven by air pressure was electrified, an improvement that boosted sales. Other mining products soon followed, and by 1900 Jeffrey's product line was well established. The first major new product came in the late 1880s when the company began the manufacture of an underground electric locomotive for hauling coal from the mine. As coal came from the mine, it was in large chunks, an inconvenience to the mining companies that needed crushed coal for the markets. Jeffrey then began the manufacture of coal crushers for sale to the mining companies. To Jeffrey's benefit, the mining companies were always ready to purchase new equipment that would improve productivity. Thus, in the 1890s, the mining companies readily acquired Jeffrey's newly manufactured conveyors that could rapidly move coal through the mine tipples. Just few years after the move to the Milo area Jeffrey's engineers designed a new drive chain for the coal cutters, and under a patent the company began the manufacture of the product. The chain had uses by other industries, and within a few years, the Jeffrey Company was earning a larger profit from chain sales than from coal cutters

Although Jeffrey Manufacturing was non-union until 1953, the founder, J.A. Jeffrey did not neglect amenities for the workers. In 1889, he established one of the country's earliest industrial infirmaries, and in 1904 set up a cooperative store, followed in 1912 by an employee cafeteria. J.A. Jeffrey took a major step in employee warfare in 1912 when he created the Jeffrey Building and Loan Association that financially assisted employees in buying a home. When the depression forced the cancellation of the program in 1930, the loan association had helped finance over 2,000 homes.

Jeffrey Acquisitions

As chain sales continued strong, Jeffrey in order to insure a reliable supply of iron casting for chain production, purchased the Ohio Malleable Iron Company in 1904. The location of Ohio Malleable, just a few blocks north of First Avenue, along the same railroad tracks on the opposite side, allowed for convenient shipping between the two companies. Ohio Malleable was never wholly integrated into Jeffrey, and throughout its long history, spanning another seventy-five years, Ohio Malleable retained its name and separate identity. This acquisition proved beneficial to Jeffrey, as helped by Mallable's castings, Jeffrey's total sales in 1908 totaled about $3.9 million with thirty percent coming from the chain and materials division.

Two other acquisitions were significant for Jeffrey's future. Tariff barriers that reduced export sales led the company in 1926 to purchase a British company, the Diamond Coal Cutter Company. Renamed the British Jeffrey Diamond Limited, its purchase price of $800,000 was recovered by 1939, thanks in part by British government war orders. Three years later, Robert Gillespie, the company's president following the 1922 retirement of the founder, J.A. Jeffrey, invested two million dollars for the purchase of Galion Iron Works, a manufacturer of road rollers and graders for sale to local and state governments. Although

Galion products were unrelated to Jeffrey's mining business, the purchase was made in order to smooth out Jeffrey's cash flow over the fiscal year.

With plunging sales, Jeffrey survived the depression of the 1930s. Its sales, for example, were two million dollars in 1932 compared to fifteen million dollars in 1920. But World War II brought increased prosperity to the company, as many of its products were useful to the military. Jeffrey's chain product was purchased in large amounts for use as ammunition hoists for navy combat ships. and its Galion road building equipment was in demand by allied construction battalions in many countries. Sales of coal mining equipment remained brisk throughout the war, as demand for coal remained constant. By 1943, Jeffrey's sales had rebounded to $23 million. Company prosperity continued into the immediate post war years, with a1948 profit of $7.4 million on sales of $68 million, nearly triple that of five years earlier. Yet the impressive sales and the company's continued national leadership in mining equipment products began to dull Jeffrey's competitive edge, as management became complacent. In the company's history written by the great-grandson of the founder quoted the 1949 family head, R.H. Jeffrey, saying at that time "we have all the business we know what to do with."

A drawing of Jeffrey Manufacturing Company at its largest physical size. Where the tracks curve at the bottom is the site of Kilbourne and Jacobs, purchased by Jeffrey. At the upper center, the large, flat-roofed building with two trees in front is the Company office, built in 1924. All the buildings in front it and over to the railroad tracks were demolished in the 1980s. The office building was saved, and a few years ago, was converted into upscale apartments. (Columbus Metro Library)

Decline

Jeffrey's decline can be traced to the late 1940s and early 1950s when the company failed to replace its underground coal hauler that ran on tracks with a rubber tire hauler, an innovation that would save the mining companies both time and money in not having to constantly build more tracks as mine shafts were extended. Jeffrey's management thus allowed its competitors, particularly the Jay Manufacturing Company, to capture the market for the new hauler. Jay also bought patent rights for a newly developed coal cutter that would both cut and load coal without using explosives. Jeffrey was not blind to these developments, but a company report concluded that the company's declining market share of the new equipment would not be extensive. Yet by the late 1950s, Jay was the industry leader in the production of mining equipment, while Jeffrey had fallen to last, which meant fourth or fifth place.

Fortunately, as Jeffrey had made its acquisitions of Ohio Malleable, Galion, and British Diamond, it permitted each company to continue to manage itself, a practice that was formalized in 1946 when Jeffrey was reorganized as a holding company, allowing Jeffrey's manufacturing division and the three subsidiaries to become operating companies. By the 1950s, the subsidiaries were carrying the once powerful manufacturing arm of Jeffrey. In 1952, for example, as Jeffrey's net income was $1.6 million, Galion's net on road equipment came to $2.2 million. For the period 1951 to 1962, the holding company's total net income was $52 million, of which $40 million came from Galion and British Diamond. A reorganization in 1961 abandoned the holding company concept, and the complete merger with Galion, resulting in the new corporate name of Jeffrey Galion, Inc.

Under the new organization, Jeffrey's consolidated sales rose to $96 million in 1963 and to $137 million in 1966. However, during this period Jeffrey's contribution to Columbus manufacturing took a nosedive, for in the early 1960s the company transferred much of its production to more modern facilities in North Carolina and Tennessee. Yet the improvement in consolidated sales did not prove to be a harbinger of a renewed future, for as will be shown later, the beginning of the end was just over the horizon.[2]

Milo-Grogan Annexation

As industry followed the railroads to the northeast of the Union Station, individuals and families in turn followed seeking employment in the growing factories. The population incursion near the new factories resulted in the establishment of the communities of Milo and Grogan, mostly within the railroad square. Milo stretched from First to Fifth avenues along Cleveland Avenue and west to the railroad tracks, while Grogan was east of Milo and before annexation extended to Eleventh Avenue on both sides of Cleveland Avenue. The name Grogan derives from John Patrick Grogan who in 1894 opened a grocery and dry goods store at 1355 Cleveland Avenue, about three blocks north of Fifth. "Milo" was taken from Milo Streets who owned a brickyard at St Clair and Third avenues. The boundaries of Milo and Grogan were never precise because neither ever had a legal or corporate existence. Thus lacking a legal framework, there were no formal barriers to their being considered as a unit, thus the unifying name "Milo-Grogan" became common. The sharing of Cleveland Avenue as their business strip further promoted the unity of the communities.

At about First Avenue, Milo-Grogan began where Columbus's corporate boundary ended, a proximity that made it natural for many Milo-Grogan residents to advocate their community's annexation to Columbus. More tangible reasons for annexation included Milo-Grogan's inability to provide for paved streets, its own water supply, a sanitary method of sewage disposal, or for reliable electricity. But Columbus authorities did not initially leap at the chance to add these communities to the city, as cost considerations made them hesitate. With respect to the Columbus School District, cost had been the basis for the board's 1896 rejection the Milo schools' request to become part of the Columbus system. When the request was made the Milo school board had recently completed a large school building on Third Avenue, incurring a $30,000 debt that the Columbus board did want to absorb.

By 1907 annexation of the land area of Milo-Grogan was coming to a head. Nevertheless, it remained true that the Columbus City Council and the politically powerful Board of Trade were not quite ready to made the leap, both bodies seeing dollar signs as they viewed Milo-Grogan's infrastructure needs. As the Columbus Dispatch pointed out in February 1907: "The streets of Milo are in a deplorable condition; it is nothing but mud, mud everywhere … The Harbor Road (Cleveland Avenue) which forms the main street through the village is almost impassable, except in the dry summer season." Moreover, as the paper explained, annexation would mean an immediate responsibility for Columbus to provide for water and sewage services. Sewage was an especially critically problem, as Milo was discharging waste matter directly into an open ditch. Adding to these expenses would be the extension of police and fire services into the annexed territory.

Milo and Grogan did of course have taxable assets that annexation would bring to Columbus. Taking the area of the Milo-Grogan school district of 622 acres, building lots over these acres were in 1907 valued at $283,000, while personal property was valued at nearly $391,000. With other taxable assets included, Milo-Grogan had a total taxable value of over $791,000.

Although cost was a critical factor in Columbus's consideration of annexation, a growing intangible factor was perhaps becoming more important. This was known as a "Greater Columbus," a concept that by 1906 was supported by many Columbus boosters including city authorities, Board of Trade members, and many sections of the public, all of whom advocated a city with a growing population and an expanding land base. Unless Columbus strove to move in this direction, the city could never be one of the country's upper tier metropolises. Thus, Milo-Grogan's advocacy for attachment to Columbus by 1907 was timely, for many in the city were already in favor of more territory.

In early February 1907, Milo-Grogan annexationists arranged a meeting at City Hall on State Street with Columbus Mayor Dewitt Badger. About forty Milo-Grogan residents attended along with Board of Trade members, city officials, and other interested parties. The meeting was something of a pep rally for annexation. One Columbus advocate stated: " I am absolutely and unqualifiedly in favor of Greater Columbus. If the people of this city play their hand for all it is worth, Columbus is destined to become the greatest inland city in these United States." A Board of Trade member said:

It is plain that the annexation project is receiving serious consideration on all sides. Most people, I think, now realize that the city must be enlarged before long. Cities grow like other things and must not be hemmed in. The mere idea of Greater Columbus is a profitable one for the city. The movement cannot be stopped now that it has started.

Again, another resident spoke up for a Greater Columbus:

And then let us add Greater Columbus! Columbus wants the additional population that Milo and Grogan and their neighbors will give her, to place her in 1910 beyond the 200,000 mark and in the class of cities where she belongs.

Milo- Grogan residents did not pick up the Greater Columbus theme, as more practical matters were on their minds. A Grogan merchant said: "In some matters we are in pretty good shape, and we do not need the city's help. But we do need better streets, sewery, and water works badly." A Grogan grocer agreed, stating:

If we don't get better streets soon, it will be as hard to find ourselves in the mud as it is Columbus to find those lost poles. We don't need your police, but we do need streets and sewers and water. Cleveland Avenue is so impassable that we don't know what a farmer looks like anymore. They all go into town some other way.

Mayor Badger summed up the meeting, stating: "This has been a grandly successful opening meeting of the annexation movement...I can almost see Greater Columbus growing by metes and bounds, and Milo and Grogan, and other contiguous territory with her."

There were, of course, Milo-Grogan residents who did not want their community to join Columbus, the principal argument against annexation being higher taxes. The opponents maintained that Milo-Grogan's problems could be handled by incorporating the community as a village, which would give it taxing authority, and therefore the resources to improve its water and sewage systems, and pave the streets.

In the winter of 1907, the township allowed Milo-Grogan residents to vote on the question of joining Columbus or incorporating as a village. In this election, the annexation supporters decisively defeated the village option by a margin of 363 to 26. The opponents, however, were able to force the township to hold another election, and in October 2008 the community again favored becoming a part of Columbus, the margin being 270 to 68.

The ball was now in the court of the Columbus City Council but, according to the Columbus Dispatch, "malcontents" were able to delay city council action for over a year. By 1910 the Greater Columbus forces finally prevailed. The Dispatch wrote that "the great mass of people were willing and even eager" for annexation. The Chamber of Commerce, successor to the Board of Trade, was supportive of a larger city, and on March 29, 1910 a unanimous city council voted Milo-Grogan into Columbus along with six other areas as part of the Greater

Columbus movement. Two days later, the Dispatch editorialized in support of the council's action: "Greater Columbus is now in sight, the last important step toward it having been taken by council when it unanimously voted to take into the city six of seven districts that were some months mapped out for annexation." Milo-Grogan added just over 1,143 acres to Columbus land area. Another of the six areas annexed was the Pennsylvania Railroad Shops, located along the railroad tracks that bordered Milo-Grogan on its southern boundary. (More on these shops below).[3]

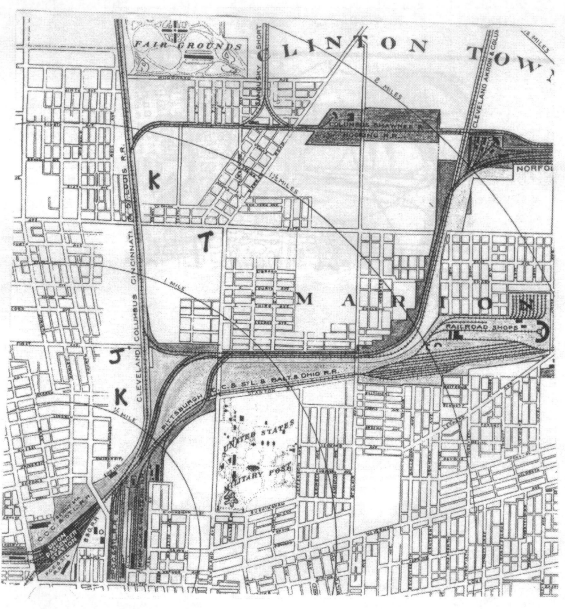

This 1893 Columbus map shows the railroad square within which Milo-Grogan was located at its annexation in 1910. Note the railroad shops to the right or east of the square. The letters J and K to the left or west of the square represent the location of Kilbourne and the future location of Jeffrey. The T and K inside the square indicate the future location of Kinnear Doors and Timken. (Columbus Metro Library)

Assets to Columbus

Following annexation, Milo-Grogan, by virtue of its over 1100 acres, became an important part of the Greater Columbus concept. However, the immediate tangible benefit to Columbus was the community's nearly $800,000 of taxable property. Given Milo-Grogan current factories and with more soon to follow, it appeared that the new community would be an economic asset to Columbus far into the future. Prior to annexation, the largest employer in the Milo-Grogan area was the Pennsylvania Railroad, their tracks extending parallel and next to First Avenue. Along these tracks and just east of St Clair Avenue was a collection of railroad shops dating from the 1880s that formed a minor industry in itself (see map above). At the time of annexation in 1910, the shops comprised a powerhouse, erecting shop, boiler shop, machine shop, paint shop, blacksmith shop, and a planing mill. Known locally as the Panhandle Shops (Panhandle was the nickname for the Pennsylvania Railroad), this enterprise along with the railroad proper employed several hundred workers early in the 20th century.

The railroad's influence in the Milo-Grogan area was not limited to its role as an employment source. It also sponsored a semi- professional football team, known as the "Panhandles," who traveled via the railroad for league play in Akron, Youngstown, and other areas of Ohio. In addition, while the future Timken lot was still vacant, the Pennsylvania was influential in bringing circuses to the lot along Cleveland Avenue.

No factory had been operating in the Milo-Grogan area as long as the Pennsylvania Railroad, but prior to the 1910 annexation two factories that would employ several workers had begun operations north of Fifth Avenue along the eastern side of the railroad tracks that became the western border of Milo-Grogan (also the same track along which Jeffrey Manufacturing was located). First to arrive was Kinnear Doors, a manufacturer of steel and aluminum doors with interlocking slats that allowed the door to be vertically raised as the slats coiled above the doorway, thereby freeing up space consumed by swinging doors. Columbus entrepreneurs W.R. Kinnear and E.B. Gager designed the door in the 1890s, and from their Milo-Grogan site, their product became enormously successful. Soon the new company had both a national and international market, as factories found the coiling doors indispensable in the loading and shipping areas. The doors were highly versatile, allowing Kinnear engineers to make custom designs, such as a twelve-story high door for a grain elevator. In another case, Kinnear designed and built a factory wall with a group of doors so than cranes could be moved within the factory as the doors were raised. The doors were also efficiently used on beverage trucks, on ships where space saving was a necessity, and as factory fire doors when closed. In the 1950s, Kinnear's Milo-Grogan plant employed about 400 workers.

In 1902, just to the north of the Kinnear plant, Ohio Malleable Iron Company acquired eleven acres, and the same year began constructing an industrial site of ten buildings. By the end of the year, the company with about 175 workers would be casting iron and steel products for Columbus metal manufacturers. Ohio Malleable was founded by former officers of the

Buckeye Malleable Iron and Coupler Company, which had been in operation since 1889 to the immediate south of Kilbourne and Jacobs. (As we will see in the next section, Buckeye Malleable was the forerunner of Buckeye Steel Castings Company that would locate on the South Side, forming the nexus of another industrial community).

Ohio Malleable Iron did not long remain an independent company. As mentioned in the discussion of Jeffrey, Ohio Malleable was acquired by the larger company in 1904. Since Jeffrey allowed Ohio Malleable to operationally function as a separate company, its manufacture of steel castings for Jeffrey's chain division assured the viability of the smaller company. In the early 1950s, Ohio Malleable employed about 540 workers. The company continued to operate under its own name at the Milo-Grogan site until 1953 when Jeffrey sold it to the Dayton Malleable Iron Company.

Just outside the 1910 annexation boundary, and thus already a part of Columbus were several factories lured by the railroad that opened in the first decade of the 20th century. Along the tracks to the south of First Avenue were the Poste Brothers Carriage Works, Morris Iron Works, Case Manufacturing Company, Ohio Elevator Machine Company, and the Columbus Malleable Iron Company. On the west side of the track square, and also already inside Columbus by 1910, the Columbus Lithograph Company had been operating. Since 1900 the Columbus Coated Fabrics Company had also operated on the west side of the railroad tracks. From its plant just across the tracks from Kinnear Doors, Columbus Coated produced oil cloth and other coated materials. A successful company for many decades, Columbus Coated employed over 1,100 workers in the early 1950s. Although these companies were not part of the 1910 annexation, they all enhanced the economic viability of Milo-Grogan, as they were a source of employment to the new community.

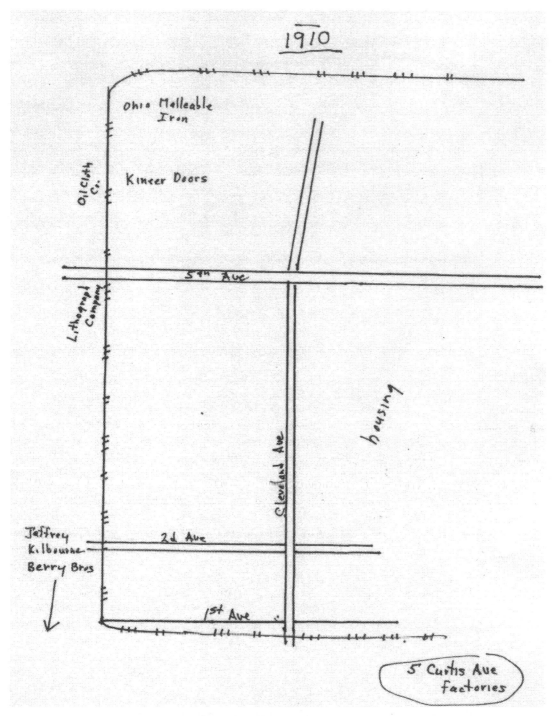

A drawing from a 1910 Columbus real estate map showing the factories in and around Milo-Grogan at the time of its annexation. (Blaist's Columbus Real Estate map is in the Columbus Metro Library.)

Assets After 1910

In the decade following annexation, two significant industrial enterprises built plants in the heart of Milo-Grogan along Cleveland Avenue between Fifth and Starr avenues. Surprisingly, this large area beginning at the intersection of Cleveland and Fifth avenues had never been developed. The lateral streets - Fourth, Gibbard, and Third – that ran east of Cleveland had never been extended across Cleveland, thus leaving the vacant area unimpeded. This undeveloped area stretched from Cleveland west to the railroad tracks (The same tracks along which Jeffrey, Kilbourne, Kinnear, and Ohio Malleable operated.) First to occupy this large area was the Columbus, Die, Tool, and Machine Company, an enterprise that produced precision tools and dies for local metal fabricating factories. Columbus Die had been established in 1906 on Naghten Street just south of the Union Station in the Irish District. Later the company relocated to Mt Vernon Avenue, from which it moved to Milo-Grogan in 1914 where it built a factory along Cleveland Avenue near Starr. This would place it directly south of the future Timken plant, where Columbus Die would remain for a half-century.[4]

The Timken Roller Bearing Company filled out much of the Cleveland and Fifth avenues open area when it began the construction of a 148,000 square foot factory in September 1919. Upon beginning operations in spring 1920, Timken had invested about four million dollars in new plant and equipment. While the new plant was under construction, Timken obviously eager to get started in Columbus began manufacturing bearings at Buttles and the Olentangy River in a building owned by Columbus Structural Steel, one of the Flytown companies.

Unlike many of Columbus's other large industrial companies, such as Jeffrey, Kilbourne, Ohio Malleable, Kinnear, and the Flytown companies, which were "home-grown", Timken came to Columbus as a branch plant of the company's principal industrial site and offices in Canton, Ohio.

A manufacturer initially of precision bearings for carriages, then for motor vehicles and railroad cars, the company was started by the German immigrant, Henry Timken. Prior to Timken's wheel bearings, patented in 1898, the problem of friction in wheeled vehicles had never been satisfactorily solved, a principal problem being the friction created while turning. But in the late 1890s, Timken and his two sons built a set of tapered roller bearings for carriages that eliminated nearly all friction. In the first years after the patent, Timken operated a factory in St. Louis, achieving success manufacturing carriage wheel bearings. About 1900 it was becoming clear that automobiles would soon displace carriages, and Timken in order to be near automobile producing sites, opened a new factory in Canton, Ohio in 1902.

In choosing Columbus as a location for a branch plant, the Timken company, as reported by Henry Hunker in his industrial history of Columbus, was impressed by the city's excellent railroad connections to wide markets and to raw material centers, as well as its abundant labor supply. As Timken opened its Milo-Grogan plant, it became an immediate economic success, as over 1,800 workers were soon employed, with growth continuing through the prosperous years of the 1920s.

Timken was justifiably proud of its product. So effective and non-resident were its bearings that a railroad locomotive could be pulled on a flat surface by three women in high heels. Timken demonstrated this in the 1930s with the Four Aces locomotive, the first train car equipped with Timken railroad bearings. The Four Aces toured the country, making stops so that the women could perform their feat for the benefit of future Timken customers.

Following the doldrums of the 1930s, World War II contracts brought increased business to Timken, and employment during the war years exceeded 5,000. When the end of the war brought an end to the profitable government contracts, Timken's civilian bearing production resumed at a steady pace, as its Columbus employment in the 1950s hovered around 4,000. Timken's future in Columbus at this point appeared bright.

The Timken Roller Bearing plant at Fifth and Cleveland avenues in Milo-Grogan in 1928. The horizontal street that angles downward is Cleveland Avenue intersecting with Fifth Avenue. Since 1996, the large plant site has been vacant surrounded by a barbed-wire fence.

After Timken began operations in its new 1920 plant, two years later Clark Grave Vault, an already successful company, relocated from the west side of the Scioto River to East Fifth Avenue, just across the railroad tracks from Timken. From its new site, just outside the Milo-Grogan boundary, Clark continued with its production of steel vaults designed to hold burial caskets in order to prevent soil and water damage to the caskets. Like many other Columbus manufacturers, Clark's principal product was stymied during World War II when the company became a defense contractor. But like Timken after the war, Clark's civilian success continued, as its vault manufacturing resumed its pre-war profitability. During the mid-1950s, Clark's employment was in the range of 800 to 850 workers.

One other company can be mentioned that was a part of Milo-Grogan's assets to Columbus. This was the Columbus Die and Tool Company, which located in 1928 on the north side of Fifth Avenue, just across the street from Timken. Always a small company of skilled workers, Columbus Die remained a local asset into the 1980s.[5]

Commercial Milo-Grogan

The economic undergirding of the community by the foregoing factories and the growth of a resident workforce led to the development of a vibrant business strip along Cleveland Avenue from First to Fifth avenues. But preceding the commercialism of Cleveland Avenue, the Columbus Central Railway Company in the 1890s had constructed a striking, two-story brick building with a steep gable roof at nearly the southern entrance to Milo-Grogan. Located on the east side of Cleveland Avenue at the intersection of Reynolds Avenue, one block north of First Avenue boundary, the building featured a tall, rounded corner tower topped with a conical, slate sphere. Had it been common at that time, this structure could have served as a gateway symbol into Milo-Grogan. But it was not promoted in such a manner, remaining entirely functional, serving as the office Central Railway Company, which in 1914 became Columbus Railway, Power, and Light Company, owner of the streetcar system.

Across Reynolds Avenue extending a block to First Avenue were two other buildings belonging to the streetcar owners – the power plant and the streetcar barn, built in 1894. Since 1891 a streetcar had ran from downtown and north on Cleveland Avenue to the barn at First Avenue where it turned around. By October 1895, after Columbus streetcars had been electrified for four year, the Columbus and Westerville Railway Company extended the route several more miles north along Cleveland Avenue to the town of Westerville. Thus, fifteen years prior to annexation, Milo-Grogan residents had enjoyed public transit through their community.[6]

Although the railway office building might have signaled the southern entrance into Milo-Grogan, travelers in 1910 should not have assumed that a business strip lay ahead, for at the time of annexation little commercial activity had as yet evolved on Cleveland Avenue. A Columbus real estate map for 1910 shows that on the east side of Cleveland from Reynolds to Fifth avenues there were fifty-six surveyed lots, but only twenty-eight had been built upon, and nearly all of these twenty-eight structures were residences. (Recall that the west side of Cleveland Avenue was primarily taken up by the large, vacant, future Timken space). Thus, by 1910 Milo-Grogan's future business strip did not have a single confectionery, restaurant, drugstore, dry goods store, or even a saloon.

As Cleveland Avenue was sparsely built upon, so were the lateral residential streets, extending east of Cleveland. Like the future business strip, these streets – Second, Starr, Third, Gibbard, and Fourth - by 1910 had been fully platted, primarily into a grid, each block surveyed into a series of narrow lots about fifty feet in width, each street meeting a cross street at a ninety degree angle. However, by the annexation date only the lots in the first three blocks from Cleveland Avenue were fully complete with a dwelling house. In the next three blocks, approaching St Clair Avenue, the lateral streets were mostly devoid of housing. Even ten years later in 1920, these lateral streets at their eastern end near St Clair had just spotty housing.

In spite of still empty housing lots, the number of workers and their families during the decade of the 1910s was increasing enough to support growing commercial activity along Cleveland Avenue from First to Fifth avenues. By 1917 this business strip sported a movie theatre, a dry goods store, three confectioneries, five grocery stories, and two saloons. In the first two blocks north of Fifth Avenue, two more groceries operated. Mingled among the commercial outlets were bout fifty dwelling houses, comprising a mixture of single-family homes, duplexes, and one apartment building. By 1920, this construction had reduced the number of vacant lots to nineteen from twenty-eight in 1910, while during the decade, many residences had been converted into businesses.

Although never as busy as Cleveland Avenue, St Clair Avenue six or seven blocks to the east would over the coming decades contain retail and other commercial outlets benefiting Milo-Grogan residents on that side of the community. In 1917, the city directory showed that on St Clair four grocery stores and five saloons were in business scattered among some thirty-five dwelling houses, all located between First and Fifth avenues.

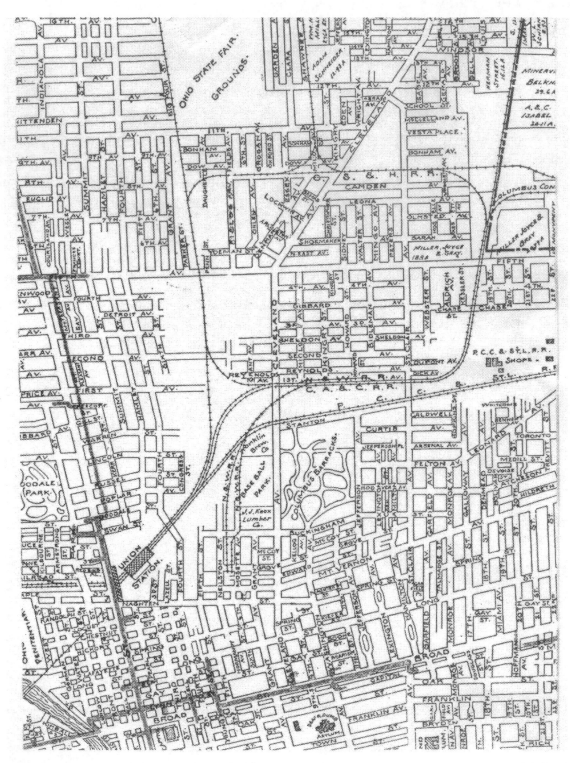

This is the same view of the 1893 map of Milo-Grogan shown earlier. This 1911 map is useful for the completed street pattern with street names. (Columbus Metro Library)

1920s and 1930s

Over the next ten years to 1927, commercialism along Cleveland from First to Fifth avenues and another two blocks north of Fifth had increased significantly. Developing in the absence of zoning that separated residential areas from commercial and industrial developments, Cleveland Avenue had become a motley mix of land uses. Of some 100 to 110 structures from First to Essex Avenue (two blocks north of Fifth) about thirty-five were commercial enterprises. These included five restaurants, six groceries, two confectioneries, two drugstores, two dry goods stores, and three shoe repair shops. In addition, two physicians, a dentist, a real estate office, a plumber, barber shop, beauty salon, tire shop, two gas stations, and a billiard parlor also served the community.

The map below identifies the retail and other businesses by block.

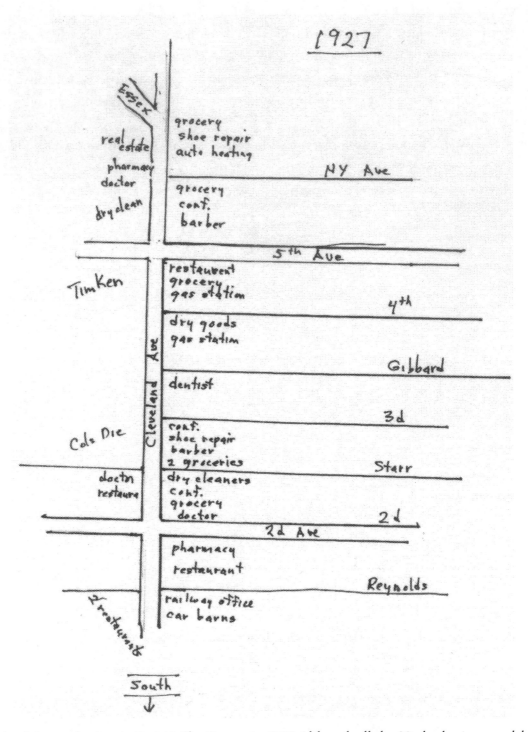

Cleveland Avenue business strip in Milo-Grogan in 1927. Although all the 30 plus business are labeled, the drawing is deceptive in that among the retail shops, there were about 100 dwelling houses along this section of Cleveland Avenue.

Between 1917 and 1927, commercial outlets on St Clair Avenue from First Avenue to the north grew from nine to seventeen, in spite of the street's five saloons of 1917 being eliminated by prohibition in 1919. Grocery stores had increased from four to eight, and the street now held a meat store, a drugstore, two confectioneries, three billiard halls, a gas station, and a soft drink store. But St Clair remained mostly as a residential street, having in 1927 about eighty dwelling houses among the businesses.

Fifth Avenue, always a major Columbus east – west through street, had long existed prior to the establishment of Milo and Grogan as communities. Within Milo-Grogan, Fifth Avenue's commercialism was principally in the three or so block area from Cleveland Avenue to the railroad tracks. By 1927 on the same side of Fifth as the Timken plant, an ice and fuel company, an automobile repair shop, and a gas station operated. Across the street from Timken, there were two restaurants and the Fifth Avenue Theatre, which near the Cleveland intersection showed motion pictures. East of Cleveland Avenue to St Clair, residential dwellings predominated, sharing this six or seven block area with two groceries, two confectioneries, an automobile repair shop, a gas station, and a Methodist church.

Given the drastic decline in Columbus's factory output and employment during the depression of the 1930s (industrial employment for all of Columbus declined by nearly 10,000 workers in the early 1930s), one might think that Milo-Grogan's retail would show a significant reduction, but such was not the case. We do not have Milo-Grogan's commercial sales volume for the 1930s, but in terms of the number of commercial outlets, there was no reduction from the prosperous year of 1927. For Cleveland Avenue, comparing the number of businesses in 1937 with those of 1927, the depression year actually shows a numerical growth, as seen in the chart below.

Cleveland Avenue		
	1927	**1937**
Restaurants	5	5
Grocers	6	6
Confectioneries	2	4
Drugstores	2	2
Dry Goods	2	4
Shoe repair	3	3
Barbers	3	6
Gas stations	3	6
	–––	–––
	26	36

The above columns show only businesses with multiple outlets. As mentioned previously, 1927 businesses totaled 35 when those with a single outlet are included. For 1937, there were an additional 10 single outlet businesses for a total of 46. All the above figures include Cleveland Avenue from First to Essex avenues. Along this part of Cleveland, there were about 119 total structures in 1937; thus businesses represented nearly forty percent of the street building volume.

Over on the eastern side of Milo-Grogan, the story was much the same as on Cleveland Avenue, as the number of business outlets on St Clair Avenue increased form 1927 to 1937. The chart below compares the two years.

St. Clair Avenue		
	1927	**1937**
Restaurants	0	5
Grocers	8	8
Dry goods	0	2
Confectioneries	2	1
Billiards	3	1
Drug Stores	1	0
Meat Market	1	0
Soft Drink Sore	1	0
Gas Station	1	0
	___	___
	17	17

The seventeen businesses in 1927 is the total for that year. For 1937 in addition to the above list, St Clair also had two icehouses, a wholesale fruit store, a barber, two automobile repair shops, and a bakery, making a total of twenty-four commercial outlets.

Industry

For all of Columbus, the value of manufactured goods produced declined from $212,000,000 in 1929 to $90,000,000 in 1932, and in the same period the number of employed factory workers fell from 26,600 to 17,600.[7] The assumption must be made that Milo-Grogan manufacturing and factory employment dropped by an equivalent amount. Yet area factories of Milo-Grogan survived the depression to experience better times during the next decade. Columbus real estate maps for 1937 show the following factories all in operation.[7]

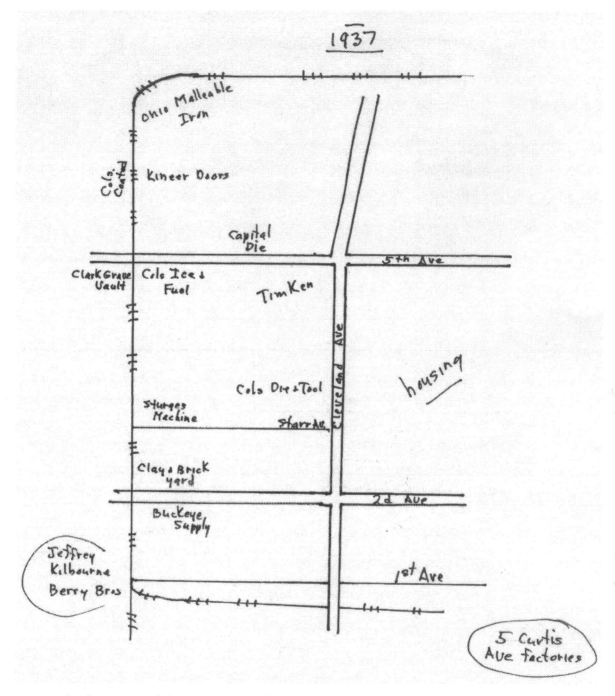

During the depression of the 1930s, the Milo-Grogan area factories survived. The drawing shows the principal factories as of 1937 that continued into the 1940s.

World War II and After

From the self-interest of the Milo-Grogan factory owners and workers, it was fortunate that their industry survived the depression decade, for boosted by war demands these factories realized increasing prosperity during the 1940s. Kinnear, Clark Grave Vault, and Timken all secured war department contracts. Timken aided by war department funds in 1942 built what would later become a railroad ball bearing plant, but during the war the new facility turned out anti-aircraft shells. Clark Grave Vault interrupted its vault production in order to fulfill war department contracts mandating production of artillery shells, armor plated hulls, navy mines, and other war materiel. Other companies, as Capital Die and Tool, and Columbus Die, saw sales increases as a result of companies with war contracts increasing their purchasing orders. Jeffrey Manufacturing already manufactured many products needed by the military, and its sales grew as the army and navy became customers.

Decline

Yet in the post World War II period when Columbus and other urban areas were basking in the prosperity of the 1950s, characterized in part by federal housing guarantees, suburban growth, and interstate highways, Milo-Grogan (even though its factories were doing well) was not participating in the prosperity. It could not because its work force was leaving the community, an event that ultimately resulted in its socio-economic statistics spirally downward. After a growth in population from 4,179 in 1930 to 4,755 in 1940, the trend then turned south at every decennial census.

Year	Population
1940	4,755
1950	4,466
1960	4,067
1970	2,869

(The above figures are for census tract 23, which covers all the area south of Fifth Avenue to First Avenue. The smaller populated area of Milo-Grogan north of Fifth is not included).

A key factor in this population decline was the large and rapid "white flight" beginning in the 1950s, leading to a reversal in the racial composition of the community. Since the 1910 annexation, Milo-Grogan had continued to be nearly an all white and working class community, as white immigrants during the 1910s populated the area. Many of these were Irish, French Canadian, and Italian. Although the immigrant influx was checked in the early 1920s, due to a change in federal immigration law, many of the second and third generations remained through World War II. After the war, as was the pattern in Flytown, the black population in Milo-Grogan began to grow in the 1940s and 1950s, the same period when whites were departing.

Many whites, as a result of military service, had veterans' benefits that allowed easy home financing. Such benefits and decent paychecks from the humming factories allowed many workers and their families to see greener grass in the white housing areas of Clintonville, North Linton, and the west side's Hilltop. Blacks, on the other hand, suffering from both and employment and housing discrimination had few choices. Unable to afford prosperous areas of the city, many began to settle in places like Milo-Grogan where housing was relatively cheap.

Thus, the combination of "white flight" and black influx of the 1950s resulted in a sea change of racial composition during the decade. Considering only the area from First to Fifth avenues, the racial change looked like this:

	1930	**1940**	**1950**	**1960**
White	3,917	3,651	3,266	963
Black	460	557	1,178	3,098

Thus, during the 1950s the white population declined by 2,303, while the number of blacks increased by 1,920. Said another way: The black population in 1950 was twenty-six percent of the total. In 1960 blacks made up seven-six percent of the total.[8] As the whites fled Milo-Grogan, they could still hold their factory jobs. The in-coming blacks may have taken over former white housing, but they did not capture white jobs, meaning community income and spending power had to decline. Thus, with both a smaller and poorer population, the retail storefronts along Cleveland and St Clair avenues could not be sustained at the levels of the 1920s, 1930s, and 1950s.

In 1957, for example, the Cleveland Avenue business strip saw a loss of twelve commercial outlets from 1937. The following chart compares the two years.

Cleveland Avenue		
	1937	1957
Restaurants	5	9
Grocers	6	3
Confectioneries	4	1
Drugstores	2	1
Dry Goods	4	1
Shoe Repair	3	1
Barbers	6	1
Gas stations	6	2
	———	———
	36	19

In addition to the nineteen businesses above, the 1957 population was still able to support a beauty salon, two car repair shops, a dime store, tools store, upholstery shop, electric appliance store, carry-out beer outlet, gift shop, radio repair shop, two used car lots, a loan company, and a pizza shop. This made a total of thirty-three businesses from First to Essex avenues. But as seen earlier, for 1937 there were nine other businesses in addition to the thirty-six above, for a total of forty-five, or twelve more than in 1957.

St Clair Avenue: A decline of businesses also occurred on St Clair from 1937 to 1957. In 1937 there were twenty-four businesses, but by 1957, only sixteen operated.

Fifth Avenue: Here the number of businesses had increased by 1957, particularly between Cleveland and St Clair avenues. In this stretch there had been four businesses in 1937. But by 1957 there were twelve including two gas stations and four grocery stores.

Interstate Effect

A second event taking Milo-Grogan down was the 1961-62 construction of Interstate 71 that extended north and south through nearly the center of the community, thereby splitting it into east and west sections. The interstate destroyed large swaths of the residential lateral streets through which movement between and Cleveland and St Clair avenues had been easily made. These severed streets were First, Reynolds, Second, Starr, Third, Gibbert, and Fourth. North of Fifth Avenue, sections of New York Avenue, Shoemaker, Leona, and Camden were bulldozed. The map below shows the I-71 path.

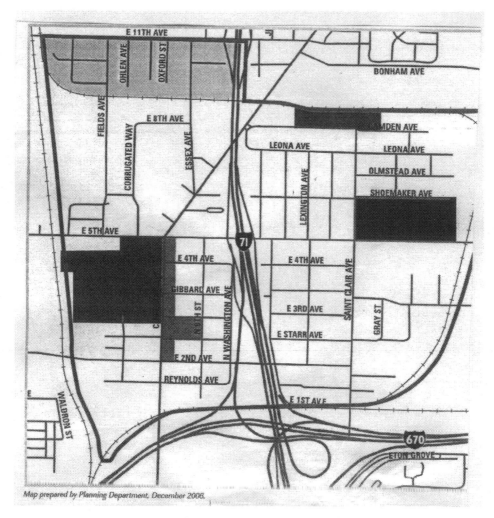

Map prepared by Planning Department, December 2006.

This illustration by the City Planning Department shows the path of I-71 through the middle of Milo-Grogan, severing all the lateral streets except Fifth and Second. The interstate was recessed under Fifth Avenue and built over Second Avenue.

Bulldozing the clearing for I-71 destroyed about 400 homes on the Milo-Grogan lateral streets. In addition, the one block north-south street named Christopher that extended between Shoemaker and Leona was obliterated. In the cleared areas to each side of the interstate, the construction crews built high, steel walls, both to block pedestrian access to the roadway and to muffle traffic noise from nearby homes. Although the purpose of these walls may have been benign, they formed an ugly "Berlin Wall" between the east and west sides of Milo-Grogan. Where there had formerly been eleven streets connected Cleveland and St Clair, the completion of the interstate reduced the number to two. Only Fifth and Second streets allowed unterrupted passage, as I-71 was recessed under Fifth Avenue and built over Second.

This contemporary photo is of the "Berlin Wall" as it looks all the way through Milo-Grogan on both side of the interstate. Although the Wall keeps pedestrians off I-71, the economic and social effect of the interstate and the Wall on the neighborhood were devastating.

The construction of I-71 through Milo-Grogan's residential section spared the physical destruction of its business strips along Cleveland and St Clair avenues. Yet in spite of their escape from the bulldozers' path, these streets soon felt the adverse impact. The destruction of some 400 homes and the removal of the residents meant a continuing loss of population. We saw that in the 1950s, the population decline was 399. In the 1960s, Milo-Grogan's population fell from 4,067 to 3,027, a loss of over 1,000 or one-fourth of the population. The adverse effect on the community's retail and storefronts was profound, as shown by comparing the 1957 businesses with those of 1967, five years after I-71 was completed.

Cleveland Avenue		
	1957	**1967**
Restaurants	9	5
Grocers	3	1
Confectioneries	1	0
Drugstores	1	0
Dry Goods	1	0
Shoe Repair	1	0
Barbers	1	1
Gas Stations	2	2
	___	___
	19	9

In addition to the above nine businesses for 1967, there were another eight from First to Essex avenues. Two of these were small used car lots and two were automobile repair shops. The other four were a dry cleaners, a carryout beer store, a refrigerator service store, and a gift shop. For 1957 as previously shown, there were fourteen other businesses in addition to the above nineteen, making a total of thirty-three, compared to just sixteen for 1967. Whereas the population loss after the interstate was twenty-five percent, the Cleveland Avenue business storefront loss was forty-five percent. With the loss of all drugstores, confectioneries, and dry goods stores, and nearly all groceries, the formerly busy Cleveland Avenue was in the post I-71 years a barren place for shopping.

The closing of the many storefronts meant vacant buildings along Cleveland Avenue, making the neighborhood decline visible to anyone passing through. By 1967, of Cleveland Avenue's sixty-five structures between First and Fifth avenues, twenty were vacant. Adding to the decaying appearance of the business strip was the condition of the once impressive office of the Columbus Railway and Light Company, which had ceased to be used by the Columbus system after 1946. It later was sold and thereafter kept in a poor state of repair. The building was never demolished, as was the adjoining car barn in the early 1950s, but maybe it should have been, given its future use. The structure that could have become Milo-Grogan's gateway site, today sits with boarded up windows and chipping paint serving as storage for an owner who cares nothing for its aesthetic quality.

St Clair Avenue: Vacant houses and buildings were also appearing on St Clair in the wake of the interstate. Of seventy structures on the street from First to Fifth avenues, eighteen were vacant by 1967. A decline from sixteen St Clair businesses in 1957 to twelve by 1967 can like Cleveland Avenue's decline be attributed to the housing destruction on the lateral streets and forced relocation of the residents. Many of the homes and businesses vacated or sold along St Clair had belonged to Italians. The Columbus city directories in the 1920s to the 1950s showed between thirty-nine and forty-nine Italian names. Then in the 1950s, the Italian names began to disappear, as this ethnic group became part of the "white flight" from Milo-Grogan. In 1957, the Italian names on St Clair had fallen to twenty-four, and by 1967, only two Italian names appeared in the Columbus directory. The Italian loss can be further seen in the closing of the ethnic lodge. In the early 1940s, the Santa Lucia Lodge was established at St Clair and Starr avenues. Later it became the Societa Fratellanza Lodge. It lasted until 1962, the year of I-71.

Fifth Avenue: Unlike Cleveland and St Clair, Fifth Avenue did not experience a business decline between 1957 and 1967. However, Fifth's businesses became automobile oriented, as nine parallel streets to St Clair Avenue were severed by I-71. Thus, as a result of increased vehicular traffic, Fifth Avenue garnered two additional gas stations and two fast food outlets in the 1960s.[9]

Social and Economic Decline

In 1973 the City of Columbus Department of Development completed a study of Milo-Grogan. (This study covered the area north of Fifth Avenue, as well as the more populated area south of Fifth, and thus the city's population statistics are larger than those used earlier, which included only the population south of Fifth Avenue). The conclusions of the city's study painted a dismal picture of the community. The social and economic conditions found were:

1) Population – a decline in the 1960s from 6,800 to 4,600. Also by 1973 one-fourth of the residents had lived in the area less than two years (many transients have little stake in the community).

2) Over one-third of the some 1,000 households were headed by a single female. This was three times the city wide rate.

3) Number of school years completed and percent of high school graduates were "well below" city wide average.

4) Unemployment exceeded that of citywide rate.

5) Mean income was one-half that of city wide mean income.

6) Twenty-five percent of Milo-Grogan families had an income below federal poverty guidelines. For city wide, the figure was ten percent.

7) For 1970, Milo students were two to three years behind the average achievement level for the rest of Columbus school system.

8) Crime – Milo-Grogan offense rate was twenty percent higher than city wide rate, and for assult and robbery the Milo-Grogan rate was double city wide rate.

The study concluded by stating: "These factors indicate that the Milo-Grogan area is at a severe disadvantage in its capacity to deal adequately with community problems." (p. 6).

The housing statistics could only add to the community's problems. The study reported a 1969 housing survey that found the following:

-- Two-thirds of all homes needed minor to major repairs.
-- One-sixth of homes were dilapidated and unsuitable for rehabilitation
-- One-sixth were classified as sound.[10]

Milo-Grogan's downward economic and social spiral was reflected in the tumbling path of the St Peter's Catholic Church that opened for services in 1896, and continued to serve the community for seventy-four years. Its setting on New York Avenue, no doubt Milo-Grogan's most aesthetically designed street was located one block north of Fifth Avenue, and as it was laid out in the late 1880s, the street extended east of Cleveland for only about three blocks. The avenue's imposing feature was a linear grassy park in the center of the street with a driving lane to each side.

St Peter's initial 1896 structure housed the church on the second floor and the parish school on the ground floor. Supported in part by many Irish and Italian immigrants, the church flourished in its early decades, reaching a membership of 750 families during the 1920s and 1930s, while about 500 children attended the parish elementary school. (Many members and school children did not live in Milo-Grogan, as the parish boundaries extended beyond the community). In 1900 a rectory was built to the west of the church, followed in 1913 by a convent on the church's east side, where about ten nuns who taught at the school resided. During its first two decades, the parish purchased several lots to the rear of the church, which extended the church property over to Fifth Avenue. On the additional property, the parish in 1929 constructed a new church building west of the rectory. With this construction, the parish complex took up most of the property on New York Avenue's south side.

However, as with Milo-Grogan, the church's prosperity began to end a few years after World War II, as the "white flight" and the changing racial composition adversely affected St Peter's As the Columbus Citizen Journal put it: "The younger scions of the old families have followed prosperity to the suburbs."

The interstate path of 1962 spared the church compound, but construction did take the eastern end of New York Avenue, leaving the convent very near the interstate right of way.

The freeway compounded the church's declining membership, and by 1967 only about 150 families were on the membership roles. Declining school enrollment had already forced the parish school's closing in June 1965. The church continued for another five years, and in May 1970, the 1896 school, the convent, the rectory, and the 1929 church were all razed.

It is common for a Catholic Church to leave its doors open or unlocked during day so that members and non-members may enter for a period of prayer and reflection. But indicative of the troubled community in which St Peter's was now located, a reporter watching the church's demolition noticed a sign on one of the church doors that read: "Keep the door closed and locked at all times. Police are watching the church."[11]

The news from Milo-Grogan continued to be dismal. In 1977 due to declining enrollment, the Columbus Board of Education closed the stately Milo Elementary School on Third Avenue, which had been educating area children since 1894. It was not a physically deteriorating building, for it had been renovated in 1922, 1954, and 1957, but enrollment had decreased from 322 in 1967 to 246 in 1971.

Factory Decline

The background to the collapse of Milo-Grogan's once bustling factories is far different than that of the commercial decline. The shrinking population and the arrival of I-71 played no role in the closing of the factories, for their markets were not in Milo-Grogan, but rather were regional, national, and for some international. Fundamental to the industrial decline were changing national trends that Milo-Grogan could not accommodate. After World War II, railroads were no longer the attraction to industry that they had been early in the century. With the building of interstate highways in the 1950s and 1960s, trucks took an increasingly larger share of factory transportation, and company management looked to the outskirts of cities along the interstates for factory sites. Milo-Grogan factories were once at the edge of Columbus with an efficient and attractive railroad network available. But by the 1950s, these factories had become inner city, and with the railroads counting for little, four and six lane highways were now wanted. Milo-Grogan, unfortunately, had no way to adjust to the new industrial transportation.

The factory collapse was not immediate, as some industrial businesses would continue for as long as three and four decades after the war, though they were gradually becoming smaller with fewer employees. Jeffrey Manufacturing was one of these, its decline beginning in the 1950s when company management failed to move against competitors who were marketing improved mining equipment. A sizable chunk of Columbus employment had been lost in the early 1960s when Jeffrey transferred much of its manufacturing to modern out of state plants. Apparently company management no longer considered the adjoining rail tracks crucial for shipments and receiving. From employing over 4,000 workers in 1953, Jeffrey's Columbus employment was down to 2,000 soon after the manufacturing transfer.

By the 1960s, the Jeffrey family, which consistently had controlled the company, appeared to lose its business energy and, according to Robert H. Jeffrey's company history, the management began to seek a buyer as a means of preserving the family wealth. By 1974, the Jeffrey Family Trust (the controlling arm of the company) agreed to sell all assets to the Dresser Industries of Dallas, Texas. The agreed upon price of $120 million cash and 416,350 shares of Dresser stock would be a comfortable financial injection into the Jeffrey Trust. At the time of the sale, Jeffrey was not hurting in a business sense. From 1968 through 1971, sales and profits in the consolidated company grew each year, reaching a profit of $11.5 million on sales of $172 million in 1971. Sales slipped in 1972, but Jeffrey's last year in business was its best financially, as sales in 1973 totaled $224 million and profits came to nearly $13 million.

For Dresser Industries, the purchase did not work out, as sales decreased under the new ownership. The visible end came in spring 1987 when Dresser demolished all thirty-three buildings on the south side of First Avenue. Dresser struggled on with the company remnant for another eight years, finding a buyer in 1995, at which time, Columbus employment had fallen to about 100.[12]

Kilbourne and Jacobs, which had been located just to the south of Jeffrey, had disappeared as an entity when Jeffrey purchased it in the early 1950s, thereby folding with Jeffrey. While Jeffrey was declining, the Columbus Die, Tool, and Machine Company, located along Cleveland Avenue, south of Timken, ceased operations in 1966. To the north of Fifth Avenue, the Ohio Malleable Iron Company that had been purchased by Jeffrey in 1902, but retained its identity, was purchased by the Dayton Malleable Iron Company in 1980. The Columbus plant was then closed, eliminating about 540 jobs. Kinnear Doors, which like Ohio Malleable, was one of Milo-Grogan's original factories at the community's annexation, was purchased in 1972 by Harsco Corporation, and in 1990 Harsco sold the door company to Wayne Dalton. Dalton moved production out of Columbus to more modern facilities, thereby removing about 175 jobs from Columbus. The Columbus Die and Tool Company, which had operated on Fifth Avenue across from Timken, closed in 1982. Columbus Coated Fabrics, a century old in 2000, survived one more year. In the mid-1950s, the company had been purring along with a workforce over 1100; then it began a slow descent and at closing employed about 450.

Clark Grave Vault still operates to this day at its Fifth Avenue site that the company purchased in 1922. Still quite viable into the 1950s, Clark in this decade employed about 850 workers. Decades later in 1992, the company was manufacturing over 40,000 vaults per year, which was enough to give Clark a nationwide market share of sixty percent. In 1990, Clark opened a subsidiary company at it seventeen acre Fifth Avenue location. Called CTL Steel, its principal purpose was to produce steel for Clark's vaults. In recent years, however, Clark has been declining, and in 2009 Columbus employment was down to about 150.

In the late 1960s and early 1970s, the future for Timken Roller Bearing Company in Milo-Grogan would appear to have been secure, for in the early 1970s, Timken invested about $7.5 million for the improvement of its Columbus facilities. Ironically, shortly after this investment, Timken's business began to decline, as American automobile companies were losing market share to foreign competitors, and by 1981 Timken's Columbus employment had fallen to about 1,850. (Recall that in the 1950s, Timken employed over 4,000.) From declining sales in the 1970s and 1980s, Timken never recovered. In December 1986, the company announced that over the next three years 450 production workers would be phased out, as Timken planned for the closing of the 1920 plant that had manufactured millions of vehicle ball bearings. After the factory closed in 1989, it sat empty until September 1996 when it was razed. Timken, however, still operated the 1942 railroad bearing plant at the Cleveland Avenue site. Producing about fifty percent of the world's railroad bearings, the plant in 1996 employed about 300 workers, and survived until 2001 when the company permanently closed it, eliminating then about 200 jobs. Timken followed to demolish this plant, leaving, leaving its Cleveland and Fifth location completely vacant.

A Ray of Hope, But No Cigar

After the 1973 Milo-Grogan study by the Columbus Department of Development that had painted a bleak future for the neighborhood, the same city department published a plan in 2007 that tried to show a ray of hope for the troubled community.[13] Between the two studies, there had been a few positive developments in Milo-Grogan. Beginning in 1987, the Greater Columbus Habitat for Humanity, with funding by churches, charities, and foundation grants, began to target some of the many vacant lots in the neighborhood as home sites for low income families. Built largely by Habitat volunteers, the new single family houses were sold to deserving families at less than market value with reasonable monthly mortgage payments. For some of the new owners, even closing costs were paid, primarily by the Columbus Housing Partnership. As of 2007, Habitat had completed and sold about ninety houses in Milo-Grogan. Many of them were located along Second Avenue, west of Cleveland. Others were built along St Clair Avenue, north of Fifth.[14]

Another plus for the community was the 1974 construction of a recreation center at the corner of Second and St Clair avenues. The building featured an art room, weight room, and gymnasium. Outside were and still are basketball courts. The grassy area has been left without design features that now characterize many urban parks. But it would serve as Milo-Grogan first and only public park. Over one-third century later in the summer of 2009, the neighborhood would get a well designed public greenspace, as the city's Recreation and Parks Department invested $260,000 to design and construct a small, but pleasant park with children's playground equipment at the corner of St Clair and Shoemaker avenues, which is north of Fifth.

Milo-Grogan arguably has had just three buildings of architecture note. As we have seen, St Peter's Church was razed in 1970, and the railway and light company office had been allowed to deteriorate. However, the third structure has been spared the fate of the other two, as the Milo Elementary School on Third Avenue just east of Cleveland found a caring owner soon after its closing in 1977. Rick Mann purchased the building, and after trying a couple of ventures with it, he turned the large, three-story former school into a studio and living quarters for artists. The new endeavor became known as MILO Arts, a non-profit, tax exempt organization. In addition to their own work, the artists along with Mann have engaged in outreach to neighborhood children by conducting workshops in such artistic skills as painting, music, and photography.[15]

Milo Elementary School on Third Avenue as it looked in 1909. It closed as a school in 1977 due to low enrollment. Presently it is the home of MILO Arts. (Columbus Metro Library).

Around the corner from MILO Arts, facing Cleveland Avenue, One Milo or RMS maintains a building whose staff provides a broad range of assistance to disabled individuals, many of whom have an artistic bent. This human services organization, licensed by the state of Ohio, has been assisting the disabled since 1987.

Yet in spite of these few twinkling stars, Milo-Grogan remains a struggling, low-income community. The Habitat housing, although making life better for many families, has not turned the neighborhood around, for the residents remain poor with limited education, living as part of a one parent family. Even with the new housing built since 1987, the 2000 vacancy rate is still excessive at seventeen percent. For houses occupied by the owners, the average value for the year 2000 was $47,500, while the city wide average value in the same year was over $140,000.[16]

The authors of the 2007 city study were aware of these statistics, but their plan does not deal with any substantive or corrective measures, for it is primarily a design study. Some of the proposals include such items as a gateway in the form of an arch across Cleveland Avenue, intersections set off with stone and brick, compatible signage for businesses, design features on the "Berlin Wall," and a park on the vacant land at St Clair and Gibbert. None of these proposals have become a reality, other than the park mentioned above, which was actually built a few blocks north of the proposal.

In the mid-1990s, as the principal Timken plant was being demolished, Milo-Grogan's business strip barely existed. Over the next decade, it did not improve. In 2007, Cleveland Avenue from Reynolds to Fifth Avenue there were just five businesses – Graves Cleaners, a used car lot, and automobile repair shop, and two fast food outlets. At the south end, near the railroad tracks where the powerhouse and streetcar barn had been, a trucking company and a plumbing business operated. As to Cleveland Avenue residential dwellings, the 2007 city directory lists just thirteen addresses where someone resided. There were in 2007 more vacant lots and boarded up structures than there were operating businesses and livable housing. The former Timken site still remains barren, and given its large size, has multiplied the dismal and dreary appearance of Milo-Grogan's "business strip" that once housed over forty business and retail shops.

Although Timken hauled way all of its building remains, leaving the huge lot "clean" in that respect, the surface was left full of ruts and broken concrete, unfit for anything except rock throwing (if one could enter the grounds). The ugliness of the site has been compounded by a heavy latticed, see through fence, topped with barbed wire that circles the entire empty space, giving the site the appearance of a poisoned brownfield.

This is the vacant former Timken site at Fifth and Cleveland avenues as it looked in January 2010.

St Clair Avenue from Reynolds to Fifth avenues had by 2007 fared no better. Its businesses had been reduced to three – a construction company office, an automobile repair shop, and a trucking company. In addition, there were four churches among the many vacant lots. By 2007, Fifth Avenue, east of Cleveland, which prior to the interstate had been mostly residential, had over the years transitioned to a street of many automobile oriented businesses in addition to two fast food outlets.[17]

In his best selling book of 1962, Michael Harrington in <u>The Other America</u> discussed depressed neighborhoods and their difficulty in improving the conditions. In paraphrase form, he wrote: Once depression hits an area, the downward spiral seems to feed off itself. Population continues to shrink, property values continue to fall, and tax base declines. As vacant housing appears, poorer, less educated people move into the cheap housing. They are usually without any civic interest and many are criminally inclined. Low paying retail of small industry may move in, but this can be seen as an exploitation of the area, taking advantage of the poor who will work for low wages. Because the people are dispirited, properties are not maintained, litter is prominent, and all aesthetic appreciation seems to disappear.

Harrington continued by quoting from a federal Bureau of Labor Statistics report, which stated: "The very fact of being an area of high unemployment as against being a prosperous area, in turn, has an influence on the kind of industries that might be attracted." Concluding, Harrington wrote that quality manufacturing generally avoids an area that has the smell of defeat.[18]

Is this the condition of Milo-Grogan?

Part III

Steelton Industrial Community

Columbus's third industrial community, located on the far south side, partly inside and partly outside the city's corporation line, has historically been associated with the steel industry. Because of the early dominance of steel manufacturing, the area near and around Parsons Avenue and Marion Road acquired the customary name "Steel Town" or "Steelton." This third factory cluster began development just before and after 1900, or about one to three decades after the first Milo-Grogan area factories – Kilbourne, Berry Brothers, and Jeffrey Manufacturing – came on line.

As a railroad network was fundamental in the location of factories along the Olentangy River and in the Milo-Grogan area, the excellent railroad connections just outside Columbus's southern boundary was instrumental to the factory development at the south end of Parsons Avenue. The map below show Columbus's rail lines shortly before the steel companies built next to them.

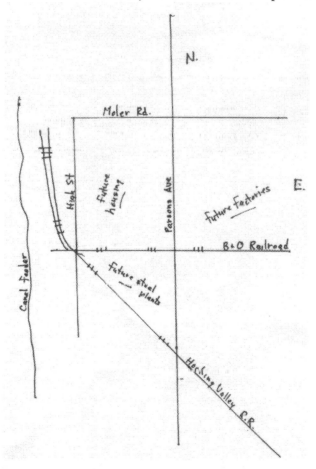

A drawing from an 1895 Franklin County map that pre-dates the steel companies. The existing rail lines of the Baltimore & Ohio and Hocking Valley railroads helped to draw the factories to this area. The rail lines continued north toward the downtown and entered into the railroad yards adjoining the Olentangy factory cluster.

In choosing the southern border area of Columbus for their factory sites, the industrialists set in motion the growth of the southern end of the South Side. The older, northern end of the South Side, bordering on Livingston Avenue, had by the first of the 20th century already developed into a viable neighborhood with a busy hub at Livingston's intersection with Parsons Avenue, which would become the "Main Street" of the South Side. Dating from Columbus's original 1812 plat, Parsons Avenue (then labeled East Public Lane) began at Broad Street, extended south across Livingston, at which point Parsons was known as Groveport Pike until about 1895 when the street was formalized as "Parsons." As the South Side developed in the latter part of the 19th century, Parsons Avenue intersected with some thirty-two cross streets from Livingston Avenue to Marion Road at the southern end of the South Side. Parsons then crossed the Baltimore and Ohio tracks and the Hocking Valley tracks, along which the future steel plants would locate, and continued into Pickaway County before its twelve-mile length came to an end. The geography of such a street, with numerous intersections and serving as an artery to a cluster of factories, all but guaranteed commercial success.

Columbus annexationists had had their eye on Parsons Avenue since the mid 19th century. From the South Side's northern boundary at Livingston, the city's first annexation in 1862 attached the street to Columbus as far south as Mithoff or about three blocks north of Frebis Avenue. This annexation also included the area west of Parsons to High Street. Annexations in 1870, 1886, and 1891 extended the city's domain over Parsons another four blocks to Moler Street, as well as adjoining areas to each side of Parsons. The 1889 and 1891 annexations captured Parsons past Marion Road and just over the Baltimore and Ohio tracks. Significantly, the southern half of these annexations gave the city only a narrow strip of land to the east side of Parsons. Behind the future storefront buildings and houses, as we will see later, factories would develop in these unincorporated tracts.

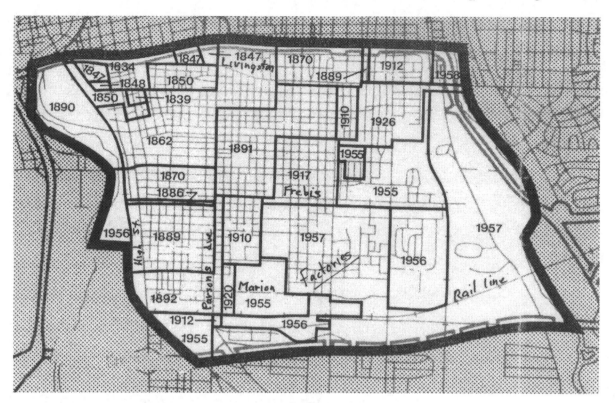

A 1973 Columbus Department of Development annexation map detailing the Parsons Avenue annexations. Note the factory sites were not annexed until the 1950s.

Primary Steel

Although steel manufacturing played a large role in Columbus's early economy, the city would become only a minor player in primary steel production, that is, the production of pig iron from iron ore. Primary steel production in Ohio become the province of huge factories in Cleveland and Youngstown, while Columbus steel plants concentrated on the fabrication of raw steel into usable products; for example, farm implements by Kilbourne, mining equipment by Jeffrey, and ball bearings by Timken. These and other Columbus factories became customers of primary steel producers in northern Ohio and Pittsburgh.

Yet the first steel plants on the South Side were in fact primary steel producers belonging to National Steel, Columbus Iron and Steel Company, and Carnegie Steel. All were located between Parsons Avenue and High Street, just south of and abutting the Baltimore and Ohio tracks, a location that put their operations outside the Columbus city limits, and therefore into the lower tax base of the township.

The year 1895 marked the first year of an operating blast furnace (a blast furnace being necessary for pig iron production) on the South Side, though this was not the first one in Columbus. That honor goes to the Franklin Iron Company, which built a blast furnace along the Olentangy River near Goodale Street in 1870, and in the early 1870s produced about fifty tons of pig iron daily. It later was moved to southeast Ohio, the source of its iron ore.

According to Henry Hunker's industrial study of Columbus, Ohio's iron ore did not match the high quality of the vast ore deposits west of Lake Superior that were shipped to steel plants in Cleveland and Pittsburgh.[1] In spite of the absence of nearby iron ore of high quality, Columbus's South Side moved ahead with blast furnace construction. The King, Gilbert, and Warner Company, operating as National Steel, completed a blast furnace at a site along South High Street and just south of the Baltimore and Ohio railroad tracks. The furnace began operating in May 1895, and was followed by a second, known as the Steelton Furnace, which had its first blast in August 1897. At eighty feet high, the second furnace had a capacity of 190,000 tons of pig iron daily. (Recall that the 1870 furnace had a capacity of just 50,000 daily.) National Steel disappears from the Columbus directories by 1903. Later maps show that its site was assumed by Carnegie Steel, which remained at High and the railroad tracks until 1920. Having two blast furnaces, a foundry, and a machine shop, Carnegie made an economic impact in central Ohio, becoming by 1918 one of Columbus's top ten industrial companies.

The Columbus Iron and Steel Company located in 1899 on eighteen acres along the west side of Parsons Avenue, the Hocking Valley Railroad tracks being to its south. It was therefore directly beside Carnegie Steel. Construction of a seventy-five foot high blast furnace for pig iron production was begun in late 1899 and completed in October 1900. A second furnace of similar size was first blown in April 1901, having the same 175,000 daily ton capacity as the first. Originally, about 300 men were required to operate both furnaces. Later labor saving devices would reduce employment by one-half. One such device was a locomotive crane installed in 1909, enabling pig iron and other material to be moved by much larger buckets. As other improvements were made, 150 men by 1920 could produce more pig iron daily than the 300 men crews of the early 1900s. The limestone needed by the furnaces came principally from quarries on the west bank of the Scioto River, which flowed south just across High Street from the plant.

In 1917, the American Rolling Mill Company (ARMCO) purchased Columbus Iron and Steel, payment being made with ARMCO stock. Production under the new owner continued for another eleven years at the Parsons Avenue site until 1928 when ARMCO moved the blast furnaces to Middletown, just north of Cincinnati. This move brought an end to Columbus's primary iron and steel industry. Henceforth, the city's steel industry would be confined to the fabrication and processing of steel.[2]

A 1915 photo of the Columbus Iron and Steel plant located at Parsons Avenue and the B&O tracks from 1899 to 1928. (Columbus Metro Library)

Other Factories South of Railroad Tracks

Other industrial entrepreneurs soon realized the tax saving advantages and the availability of inexpensive farmland beyond Columbus's corporation line. One of the first was the Chase Foundry and Manufacturing Company, which located along the east side of Parsons Avenue in 1896, just across Parsons from Buckeye Steel's future plant. A small but long lasting enterprise, the company was founded by Sherwood Chase and was first known as the Chase Pump Manufacturing, as its first product was water well pumps, but after its 1897 incorporation, it assumed its long lasting name.

An adaptable company, Chase moved into the production of brick making equipment, and then to casting steel for manufacturers of heavy duty trucks and material handling equipment. A fire in 1918 destroyed the much of the plant, but Chase rebuilt, and in 1925, was prosperous enough to enlarge the facilities. Never a large employer, even during the busy World War II years, Chase employed just over 100 workers in 1947, and by 1953, employment had fallen to about seventy-five.

In 1898, the Seagrave Corporation, a manufacturer of fire trucks and fire equipment, relocated from West Lane Avenue in Columbus to South High Street, south of the Baltimore and Ohio tracks, becoming a close neighbor of the primary steel factories. From this location, Seagram became the nation's largest manufacturer of fire trucks and accessories, a position, however, that did not make the company one of the city's larger employers. In 1929, Seagrave employed about 300 workers, one of which was an artist who hand painted all the decals and lettering on each truck. During the 1930s depression, employed fell to 145, but the company rebounded during the war years, and by 1953, Seagrave had about 310 men and twenty women on the payroll. A partial reason for Seagrave's relatively low employment was its practice, unlike the automobile companies, to build a truck only on order, thereby avoiding an inventory. Custom built trucks were a necessity due to the different specifications wanted by the many fire departments for their trucks, such as length, pumping capacity, or ladder length. Seagrave purchased its needed cast parts from local steel plants, but for its raw steel, the company had to order from Cleveland and Pittsburgh. Some of Seagrave's innovations over the years included the aerial ladder and in 1912, the motor driven, water pumping engine, allowing customers to chose a pumping capacity from 400 to 1,200 gallons of water per minute. Such improvements kept Seagrave in the forefront of truck manufacturing, thereby insuring its profitability. In 1929, for example, sales revenue was over $750,000, allowing the company to pay out dividends of over 150,000.[3]

A truck manufactured by Seagrave at its South High Street plant in Steelton. (From company website.)

Buckeye Steel

Although the primary steel companies had a significant economic presence in the early history of Steelton, their impact was limited to less than three decades. Of the fabricating steel companies and the other South Side companies, the Buckeye Steel Castings Company became the most dominant and cast the largest economic glow over Steelton and the South Side in general. When Buckeye located to the South Side in 1902, it was already a two decade old company, having got its start in 1883 as part of the burgeoning Milo-Grogan area factory cluster. For its first twenty years, Buckeye's five-acre site was located about a half-mile northeast of the Union Station and just south of Kilbourne and Jacobs along the same rail line. While at its initial location, the small struggling partnership, controlled by William

Goodspeed, was known as the Buckeye Malleable Iron Company, surviving by selling its iron products to local customers in the tool, fence, and nail business. [4]

About 1890, Buckeye insured its future success by beginning the manufacturing of an automatic coupler for railroad cars, which for the next seven decades would be its almost exclusive product. Prior to this invention, railroads used the "linch and pin" coupler, a dangerous device for trainmen who had to stand between railroad cars in order to manually couple them together. The following year after its decision to switch production, Buckeye secured a large order for the new coupler from the Baltimore and Ohio Railroad, which used the nearby Union Station for its train connections.

The success of the automatic coupler was assured in 1893 when the United States Congress passed an act requiring all railroads in interstate commerce to use the new device. As Buckeye Malleable began to prosper through the sale of the now mandated automatic coupler, the company began to outgrow its five acres on the northeast edge of Columbus, leading to Goodspeed's purchase of a large site at the city's southern edge that would allow for the construction of facilities needed for the manufacture of steel couplers. The old plant could cast only the iron coupler, and to accommodate the increasingly heavier railroad cars, steel couplers had to be manufactured.

The area just outside the Columbus corporation line had several advantages for Buckeye. The tax rates were less than that of Columbus's, the railroad connections as we have seen were excellent, and the farmland was relatively inexpensive to buy. The company's 1899 purchase of thirty-one acres along Parsons Avenue near the tracks of two railroads was therefore seen as a good investment. Moreover, the new site had the added attraction of available adjoining land that over the years would provide Buckeye with ownership of over 250 acres. Construction soon began on four buildings, one 860 feet by 125 feet and another 525 by 80 feet, which together would house three open-hearth furnaces and several cranes. A third building of three stories would serve as the machine shop, while the fourth would house the boilers and engine room.

The new factories began operation in October 1902, becoming known as the South Plant, since the original plant operated until 1910. As new facilities were added to the Steelton site, the number of open-hearth furnaces increased to five by 1905. Two additional buildings were added in 1908, expanding by 200,000 square feet Buckeye's operating area. The move to South Columbus became an immediate success, as coupler sales began a steady climb. Upon incorporating, the officers felt a name change was in order, and in October 1903, the firm became the Buckeye Steel Castings Company, a name that would last until 1967. Within the first decade of its Steelton operation, Buckeye had become the third largest coupler manufacturer in the country. The following chart details the top five producers.

Couplers sold in the U.S. 1908-1912		
Company	# Sold	% of Sales
National Malleable	1,605,000	46
Am. Steel Foundries	786,000	23
Buckeye Steel Castings	513,320	15
Gould Coupler	447,000	13
Monarch Steel Castings	93,000	3

During the years 1906 to 1914, Buckeye's monetary sales averaged over $2.3 million annually, yielding an annual net profit of about $340,000. These figures allowed Buckeye to invest $450,000 in plant improvements for 1912. Growing sales demanded a larger workforce, and by 1916, Buckeye employed over 2,000 workers, up from 400 in 1904, giving the company a significant economic impact on the South Side.

A 1957 aerial view of the Buckeye Steel works. The road near the bottom of the photo is Parsons Avenue. (Columbus Metro Library)

Buckeye's influence was social and educational as well as economic. Through World War I, the company teamed with the YMCA on the South Side to offer classes in accounting, mechanical drawing, and electricity for its employees seeking advancement. For its many immigrant workers, Buckeye sponsored "Americanization" classes for those wanting citizenship.

Like Jeffrey Manufacturing, Buckeye in its early, non-union years practiced welfare capitalism by instituting several worker benefits. In 1903, a medical officer was assigned to the factory, followed in 1915 by an on-site emergency hospital staffed by company physicians. In the same year, the company built an employee kitchen and provided locker rooms. Beginning in 1917, life insurance was provided to all plant workers after two years of service. One of Buckeye's larger worker benefits came in 1917 when the company spent $143,000 to buy 108 acres opposite the steel plant on which Buckeye built housing for its workers.

Always the Achilles' heel of Buckeye Steel, at least until the company began to diversify in the 1960s, was its total dependency on the railroads for the sale of its single major product, the automatic coupler. Moreover, its railroad sales were confined to a small number of rail lines. In 1916, for example, eighty-six percent of all sales came from just six companies. Other products marketed to railroads, such as steel wheels and box side frames, were largely failures, yielding little revenue. Nevertheless, Buckeye had some very good early years, prospering during the World War I years with sales of nearly $10,000,000 in both 1917 and 1918. However, when railroads reduced their purchase of cars during the 1921 recession, Buckeye's sales revenue plunged from about $960,000 in 1920 to less than $150,000 in 1921, resulting in a net income loss. Attempts to purchase other steel casting companies failed. To cut costs, Buckeye had some success with vertical integration. As early as 1906, the company had acquired natural gas fields to fuel operations, and before World War I, Buckeye purchased a large limestone quarry in Clark County, Ohio. However, Buckeye could never control its supply of pig iron, being dependent on Pittsburgh plants.

Into the 1920s, Buckeye continued to improve its plant efficiency in order to reduce costs. In 1923, the company invested $830,000 for building and equipment upgrading. Throughout the rest of the decade, Buckeye put another $395,000 into plant and equipment, of which $170,000 was for the installation of waste heat boilers that captured heat from furnaces and recycled for other plant uses. However, the 1920s saw no new products and no acquisitions, but net income held up, reaching $1.2 million in 1929. This cushion was needed, for the depression years of 1931 and 1932 brought a negative net income, as Buckeye followed the downward economic path of the railroads. For the balance of the 1930s, only the year 1938 ended with a loss.

Because of steel demands of World War II, the War Department was willing to partially fund plant expansion for Buckeye. At a cost to the army of $950,000 and $884,000 to Buckeye, 460 feet was added to the foundry building, 300 feet to the finishing building, while other buildings were modified. These improvements enabled Buckeye to produce 1,000 tons of cast steel armor, most of which was used for tank turrets. Although the war contracts strengthened Buckeye's finances, they could not of course permanently diversify the company. Even before the war's end, Buckeye in 1944 returned to principally producing for the railroads, but by the 1950s, railroads were a declining industry, which cast a shadow over the company's future.

Marion Road Factories

Marion Road to the north side of the railroad tracks and extending east from Parsons Avenue was the spine that connected another group of Steelton factories. Combining years, one could count upwards of fourteen factories in the first third of a mile from Parsons Avenue, but at any one time, the maximum number was about nine. The largest of these was the Federal Glass Company, the official address being 515 Innis Avenue, the next street north of Marion, but its large site and plant extended back to Marion Road. In 1920, Federal Glass's adjoining neighbor to the east was the J.W. Brown Manufacturing Company, and to Brown's east after 1925 was the Linde Products Company.

Across the street and fronting the south side of Marion Road were from Parsons Avenue the Hercules Box Company, Buckeye Stamping Company, Bonney-Floyd Steel Castings Company, Brightman Manufacturing Company, and the Simplex Machine Tool Company. Not fronting Marion, but directly behind Hercules was the Steelton Lumber Company. The map below illustrates their locations.

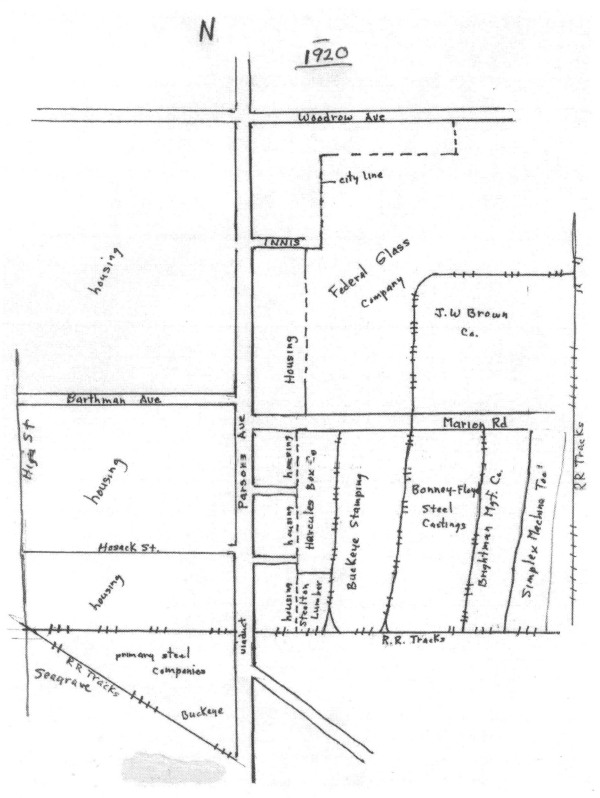

A drawing made from a 1920 Columbus real estate map showing the concentration of factories along Marion Road, as well as the steel factory sites south of the railroad tracks.

Federal Glass: Having the largest land area of the factories north of the railroad tracks, Federal Glass Company became a major player in the development of Columbus's third industrial community. Founded by experienced glass workers from Toledo in 1904, the organizers were attracted to Columbus because of central Ohio's large natural gas fields at the turn of the century. The South Side specifically was appealing due to the inexpensive farmland and the nearby railroad lines of which the company became a major user. Furthermore, the South Side location must have been sealed when the company learned that the township would abate the property tax. As we noted above in the annexation discussion, the Columbus corporation line was just in back of the Parsons Avenue storefronts, which meant that all the Marion Road factories were outside the city, and thus avoiding the higher property tax.

With available land around its Innis Avenue site, Federal Glass over the years was able to expand its production facilities through the purchase of additional acreage. By 1950, the company had twenty-three acres, which grew to thirty-five acres by the mid-1960s. Over its nearly eight-decade life span, Federal Glass was an innovative company, perfecting in 1917 an automatic feeder that rapidly weighed and separated a blob of molten glass for pressing into a forming machine. Later the company perfected continuous tank furnaces that could produce about 500,000 pounds of molten glass daily. In the 1960s, Federal Glass invested $600,000 in a 150-foot high, automatic batching facility that accepted railroad carloads of sand, ash, and lime and then releasing it in specified amounts as the materials were blended. The company became so automated after World War II that it operated seven days a week, twenty-four hours per day, a major reason being that it would be too costly to shut down and restart

Early on Federal Glass became a prime source of jobs in Steelton. In 1918, when four of Columbus's ten largest industrial employers were located in Steelton, Federal Glass was one of the four. By the early 1950s, the company employed over 1,000 workers, and in the early and mid 1960's the employment figure was over 1,300, resulting in an annual payroll of over $8.1 million. Federal Glass's local economic impact can be further appreciated by noting its heavy purchasing from Columbus suppliers, which in 1964 totaled about two million dollars.[5]

Brown Manufacturing Company: Located next to Federal Glass fronting the north side of Marion Road was the J.W. Brown Manufacturing Company, a manufacturer of lamps and lights for carriages and later for automobiles. Brown began operations in Columbus in the early 1890s near Naghten and High streets, conveniently located near the Columbus Buggy Company, a major purchaser of Brown's lamps. In the latter 1890s, Brown secured a downtown factory near Town and Fourth streets, and remained there until 1913 when the company moved to Marion Road to join the growing number of factories in Steelton. This move meant that Brown would no longer be paying Columbus taxes. At the time of the Steelton relocation, the carriage industry was near death, and Brown's principal customers were the automobile companies.

Hercules Box Company: Conveniently located just across Marion Road from Federal

Glass was the Hercules Box Company, which supplied boxes and packing material for the glass company. Opening in 1911, Hercules was more than just the local glass company supplier. Having 100,000 square feet of factory space, Hercules manufactured corrugated containers for a national market. Sales were brisk in its early decades, which led to a 60,000 square-foot expansion in 1949. In addition to manufacturing containers of pre-determined sizes, Hercules also tailored boxes to suit customer needs. By the 1950s, Hercules had become a national leader in the corrugated container industry, and in the early 1960s, employed about 300 workers.

Buckeye Stamping Company: On Hercules' east side was the Buckeye Stamping Company, which had begun business in downtown Columbus in 1902, and moved to Marion Road in 1910. In addition to saving taxes, the company's move was motivated in order to be near Federal Glass, a large customer that contracted with Buckeye to provide lettering and other designs for its glassware. Buckeye Stamping was one of the few Steelton companies that did not make use the railroad lines. Since its shipments were too small to fill a rail car, the company found it cheaper to ship by truck. Buckeye's largely unskilled workforce was not large. In the early 1950s, the company employed about fifty-five, one-fourth of these being women.

Bonney-Floyd Company: A steel casting company like Buckeye Steel, Bonney-Floyd was always much smaller, but still made a large impact in Steelton with several hundred workers. Located on Marion Road beside Buckeye Stamping, Bonney-Floyd opened in 1904 on a seventeen-acre site. (Recall that Buckeye Steel opened with thirty-one acres.) Never a manufacturer of the railroad coupler, Bonney-Floyd made a wide variety of steel castings for agricultural and mining equipment companies and for power shovel companies. After World War II, Bonney-Floyd was skilled enough to serve the aerospace and nuclear power industries. In 1953, the company's employment was about 525. (Buckeye Steel at the same employed 1,861.)

Brightman Manufacturing Company: Brightman's 1895 location on Marion Road made it one of the earliest manufacturers in Steelton, beginning operations about the time of the primary steel companies. Brightman's product of bolts and nuts for railroads and farm equipment companies did not require a skilled or large workforce, nor was it ever a large one. In the early 1950s, Brightman employed about sixty-five.

The final Marion Road manufacturer as the factory lineup looked in 1920 was the Simplex Machine Tool Company, which was located next to Brightman. Simplex was a short-lived business that began operations in 1915 and closed in 1922.

By the late 1910s and early 1920s, the Steelton factory cluster, as just outlined on both the south and the north of the railroad tracks, had become dense and concentrated, and at this time was a major source of jobs for Steelton and South Side residents. The Steelton area was clearly

Tom Dunham

Columbus's steel leader and home to a higher proportion of major manufacturing companies than other areas of Columbus. Hunker's industrial history of Columbus provides a list for 1918 of the ten largest industrial employers in the city, four of which were in Steelton. These are: Buckeye Steel Castings, Carnegie Steel, Federal Glass, and J.W. Brown Manufacturing. After the brief recession of 1921, most of Steelton's factories thrived through the 1920s, and though dented during the 1930s depression, the factories survived the decade.

In 1937, the Marion Road map for 1920 shown above would need but few alterations. Simplex Tool was gone, as noted. Replacing Simplex at the eastern end of the factory row were the Lattimer Stevens Company, the American Lathe and Press Company, and the Brown Steel Company. The largest of the three was Lattimer Stevens, a manufacturer of heating and cooling equipment, which began operations in 1920 and relocated to Steelton in 1927 and became a steady employer through the 1950s, having ninety workers on the payroll in 1953. In 1938 the company that would soon become Columbus's largest heating and cooling manufacturer located on Marion Road within a block of Lattimer Stevens. This was the American Blower Company. In addition to making air conditioning equipment, American Blower also produced dust collectors and drives for refrigerators. In the early 1950s, the company employed about 470 workers. The Linde Air Products Company, as noted above, opened in 1925. Linde was never a large employer, but it survived longer than most of its large neighbors, as it lasted until the early 1990s.[6]

We will pick up the decline of the Steelton factories after a consideration of Steelton's worker housing and retail establishments.

Worker Housing

Like the industrial communities of Flytown and Milo-Grogan, Steelton economically functioned as a single entity. The factories provided employment, the workers lived nearby, and supported the retail that developed near the residential areas. In Steelton the worker housing was largely on the west side of Parsons Avenue, extending about nine blocks to High Street. How far north Steelton extended from the factories was never defined by Columbus authorities, for the term was one of custom and not a legal geographical district. Morris Schottenstein, of the prominent South Side merchant family who knew Parsons Avenue as well as anyone, defined Steelton as extending from the steel plants north to Woodrow Avenue, noting that these six or seven blocks of Parsons Avenue contained a high concentration of retail and other commercial establishments.

Worker housing as distinct from the Parsons Avenue shops no doubt extended farther north than Woodrow. Columbus Dispatch writer Betty Daft, who studied the area, considered the area to Markison Avenue, another six or so blocks north of Woodrow, all a worker housing area. However, the statistics to be given here will use Woodrow Avenue as Steelton's northern boundry.[7]

84

Well into the 1890s, Steelton housing was in its infancy, as industrial employment had not as yet begun its growth. The 1895 map below shows Steelton as well as the larger area to Moler Road as still divided into large sections of agricultural land.

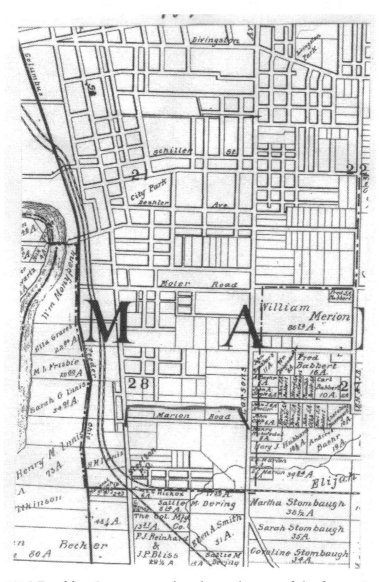

A section from an 1895 Franklin County map that shows the area of the future Steelton housing area as unplatted at this date. This is the area near the bottom from about Marion Road (this part was later renamed) to the railroad tracks. The map shows all of South Parsons north to Livingston Avenue. (Columbus Metro Library)

But just four years later, Blast's detailed real estate map for 1899 (a very large map at Columbus Metro Library, not here shown) shows the area south of Moler Road as nearly all platted into building lots fronting on laid-out streets. Only about a half-block on Hosack, Barthman, Innis, and Woodrow are shown as unplatted. However, platting does not mean a lot has been sold or built upon. Of some 650 lots, between Parsons and High Street and from the railroad tracks to Woodrow (the Steelton area), in the year 1899, less than one-half of these contained a dwelling house.

A decade in a new and growing area can make a significant difference. Thus by 1910, based on detailed real estate maps, the unplatted areas had been increasingly surveyed. Only two areas remained clear – a small area fronting Hosack Street that could hold about fourteen lots and a section between Innis and Woodrow avenues large enough for about twenty-eight lots. The west side of Steelton now had some 870 building lots, about 200 more than in 1899. More significant than the total lots, however, was that in 1910, about eighty percent of the lots contained a house, compared to less than one-half in 1899. Over the next decade, that is, to 1920, platting from Parsons Avenue to High Street was completed, except for a small section fronting Hosack Street, near the railroad tracks. Of about 900 lots, the population had grown to the point that less than 100 in 1920 were devoid of a house or other structure.

Steelton to the east side of Parsons Avenue was another matter. Here, residential dwellings were more limited, for many factories had located behind the lots facing Parsons, leaving an area large enough for only about fifteen building lots extending from the rear of the storefronts. By 1910, there were eight rows of fifteen lots between Marion Road and Woodrow Avenue, giving the eastern side of Steelton about 120 building lots, of which fifty were not built upon. As mentioned earlier, the 19th century annexations that brought to Columbus large chunks of land west of Parsons (to High Street) included only a narrow strip of land to the east of Parsons in Steelton. It was not until the 1950s that the city of Columbus began to annex significant land east of Parsons on its south end. One might assume (it is not a certainty) that the manufacturing corporations, while enjoying prestige and economic clout in the early part of the century, were able to block annexation in order to avoid paying Columbus's higher property tax. It was not until the companies were declining and losing influence that Columbus authorities annexed this land area.

Although the area from Parsons west to High Street was overwhelmingly residential, the absence of zoning allowed a few retail outlets to spring up among the residences. According to "South Side: A History," the presence of the streetcar route across Barthman Avenue from Fourth Street to Parsons influenced the growth of commercialism along the route. By the early 1910s, this "streetcar line was lined with commercial establishments from grocery stores to bar…"[8]

Other residential streets also had commercial nodes. By 1910, a grocery had opened on Reeb Avenue, one block north of Barthman. Also at this time on Innis Avenue, a grocery, two saloons, and two barbers were open for business. Another barber served customers on Hosack Street. In the 1920s, more retail opened on Innis Avenue at its western end. In this decade, a pharmacy, and A&P grocery, and a laundry were open near High Street. About midway between High and Parsons, a Kroger grocery served nearby residents. Such businesses, however, distracted little from Innis Avenue's residential dominance, as it had over 100 private homes in 1925.[9]

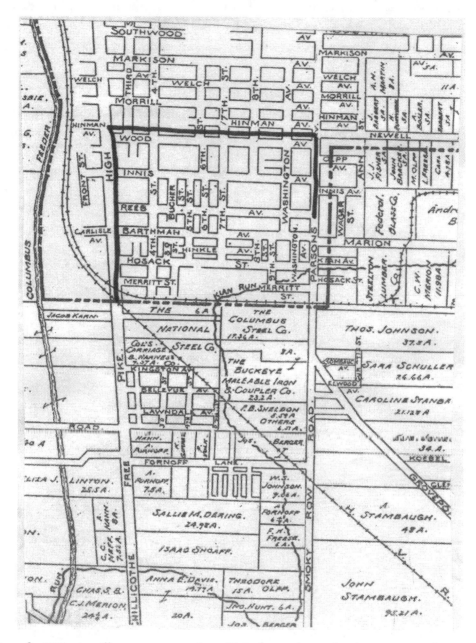

This section of a 1911 map illustrates two points: (1) It shows the worker housing area from Wood south to the railroad tracks as well platted. Compare with 1895 map immediately above. (2) Note the broken line to the right of Parsons Avenue. This is the city boundary line, outside of which the Marion Road factories were built, thereby avoiding city tax. (Columbus Metro Library)

A 1973 study by the Columbus Department of Development concluded that Steelton housing constructed between 1890 and 920 "… was built in the typical Midwest American tradition of wooden frames on narrow lots. The style of housing was somewhat the result of a combination of the earlier Queen Anne style with that of the turn of the century colonial revival. The development of housing at this time was largely the result of developer speculation seeking to capitalize on the housing demand created by expanded job opportunities."[10]

The workers and their families on the authority of Morris Schottenstein kept their homes in a good state of repair. With reference to the 1940s, Schottenstein wrote in his family history:

> These houses were typical of the homes of blue collar workers of that day. They were well maintained, usually in good painted condition with groomed yards. There were no signs of urban decay. The typical house was two-storied with a wide front porch, topped by a portico roof. Most houses had the usual format of a living room downstairs with a side stairway leading up to three bedrooms. In looking up at such a house, one would see the omni-present front room window and two smaller windows upstairs, equally distanced. Southward the homes became less expensive, but nevertheless of the same good state. There were houses on Reeb and Barthman Avenues that were well painted with groomed yards. At times, there were more doubles, and the yards were smaller with less shrubbery, but there was that sense of owner's propriety.[11]

Much of the Steelton housing was occupied by first generation immigrants. Like Flytown, the South Side was a point of entry for the country's new arrivals from Europe between 1890 and 1920. As these immigrants settled into an area, a 1921 neighborhood study of Columbus by McKenzie (referred to earlier) found that individuals of common ethnicity tended to congregate their housing in order to live as neighbors. The study found this to be especially true in Steelton, writing "this is a motley district, practically every street represents a different racial national aggregation." Writing of Steelton in 1979, Dispatch reporter Betty Daft also called attention to the immigrant ethnic group practice of living near one another. Interviewing older residents, she found that the Hungarians generally lived along Reeb, Innis, and Woodrow avenues, while the Croatians and Czechs congregated in the first block of Barthman Avenue. The Italians lived farther west on Barthman and on Fifth and Sixth streets, which intersected with Barthman. The Lithuanians and Serbs were generally found on Hosack Street, and on Morrill and Hinman avenues. A part of Hosack Street was also home to a small community of American blacks.[12]

The concentration of ethnic groups on one or two streets led to the establishment of ethnic oriented churches. The Hungarians in the first two or three decades of the 20th century comprised the largest immigrant community in Steelton, leading the Columbus archdiocese to recognize a need for a separate national parish. Accordingly, the St Ladislas Church for Hungarians was completed and dedicated in 1908 on Reeb Avenue at Eighth Street. A parish house opened in 1911, followed by a parish school in 1916, and soon after by a convent for the Ursuline Sisters who taught at the school. The Protestant Hungarians were also numerous, and in 1913, they founded the Hungarian Reformed Church on Woodrow Avenue, just two blocks from St Ladislas. Both churches have continued to be well maintained and survive today.[13]

The first two decades of the 20th century saw other institutions forming in the Steelton area. The growth in population meant the opening of schools, and in 1907, the Columbus Board of Education opened the Reeb Avenue Public School, across the street from the parish school, and educated elementary age children until 2008 when it closed.

Ethnic lodges were of course popular social centers, helping to promote close relationships and to acclimate new immigrants, while stabilizing the neighborhood. Two prominent ones were the Croatian Hall on Reeb Avenue and Ivanoff Hall on Parsons Avenue near Barthman. Croatian Hall still stands, though unused and boarded up. The once large Ivanoff Hall no longer survives, but it had been built with a bowling alley on the first floor, a dance hall on the second floor, and a stage where the Hungarian Drama Club gave performances.

A popular park for Steelton residents was Heimandale Grove on Groveport Pike, a short distance from Buckeye Steel. Opening in 1910 with picnic grounds, a dance pavilion, and later a movie area, it was a popular summer entertainment center. The Steelton Merchants Association each summer sponsored a free picnic and entertainment for children of the area. By the 1940s, the Grove had been sacrificed for a housing development.[14]

Buckeye Steel financially supported many Steelton and South Side social endeavors. In 1912, the company gave $500 to help start the development of the South Side Settlement House on Reeb Avenue, and other contributions were made to the Settlement House in subsequent years. From 1916 to 1921, Buckeye contributed $20,000 to the YMCA and the WWCA including securing a site for the South Side Industrial YMCA near the railroad tracks and Hosack Street. This was followed by another $7,500 to the YMCA in 1923.[15]

Parsons Avenue Retail

Concurrent with the growing worker housing, retail and commerce made their appearance on Parsons Avenue, becoming the capstone to industry and worker housing that formed the triad making Steelton the close and vibrant industrial community for about six decades. The commercial sparkle of Steelton can not only be explained by the concentrated worker housing area adjacent to Parsons, but also by the presence after 1916 of the Schottenstein Department Store at Parsons and Reeb Avenue, which became a shopping magnet that had a positive spin-off effect on other Steelton retail. (More on Schottenstein's below.)

The initial growth period of Steelton's commercialism arrived in the decade 1900 to 1910. Real estate developers casting an early eye at the steel and other factories coming on line began in the latter 1890s to plat lots along the west side of Parsons Avenue. (The east side would be later.) By 1899, a detailed Columbus real estate map showed the stretch of Parsons from Hosack Street, near the railroad tracks, north about six blocks to Woodrow Avenue well platted with forty-nine building lots, which at this early date fifteen had been built upon. The breakdown by block looked like this:

Hosack to Barthman ---- 4 of 15 lots built on

Barthman to Reeb ------- 2 of 10 lots built on

Reeb to Innis ------------ 4 of 10 lots built on

Innis to Woodrow -------- 5 of 14 lots built on

However, the fifteen structures built did not signal a commercial splurt, for most of the fifteen were dwelling houses, not retail shops. Unfortunately, Columbus city directories prior to 1917 did not in the street address listings distinguish between a commercial storefront and a private home. However, the directories' business section that categorizes businesses by function not by street, one can extract Parsons Avenue businesses, if there were any. City wide, the common neighborhood businesses in 1899 were grocers, confectioneries, restaurants, dress making shops, and saloons, the top two by quantity being grocers and saloons. For Parsons Avenue in Steelton, the business listings yield one saloon and none of the others. In the absence of the common businesses, except for one saloon, it appears that by 1899, commercialism had not yet achieved a foothold in Steelton. The east side of Parsons was even more barren, as it by 1899 was still unplatted.

1910

By 1910, the paucity of Steelton's commercialism had begun to turn upward. Retailers took note of the housings plats being surveyed behind Parsons Avenue and began to open shops along the avenue, judging that the area would be ripe for sales as factory workers and their families moved into the developing housing area. At the end of the century's first decade, building lots had increased to fifty-seven on the west side of Parsons, and the number of structures built on them had more than doubled to thirty-four. Significantly, the east side of Parsons had over the decade been platted into forty-seven lots, of which twenty-nine had been built upon. The breakdown by block looks like this:

West Side of Parsons, 1910	East Side of Parsons, 1910
Railroad to Hosack -------5 of 7 lots built on	Railroad to Marion ---- 13 of 18 built on
Hosack to Barthman ----- 10 of 15 lots built on	Marion to Innis -------- 12 of 20 built on
Barthman to Reeb -------- 3 of 10 lots built on	Innis to Woodrow ----- 4 of 9 built on
Reeb to Innis -------------- 7 of 11 lots built on	
Innis to Woodrow -------- 9 of 14 lots built on	

Among the sixty-three structures detailed above on both sides of Parsons, many would still be residential dwellings, but by 1910, retail shops were making an impression. The major categories, which would comprise nearly all the retail, are the following:

Saloons ------------- 12

Barbers ------------ 6

Grocers ------------ 5

Dry Goods -------- 3

Confectioneries -- 3

Drug Stores ------- 2

In addition, there was one jewelry store, one restaurant, and one furniture store.

1920

Over the next ten years to 1920, growth continued as business conditions in Columbus remained favorable and World War I demands added to factory production and employment. By 1920, the surveyed lots on the west side of Parsons in Steelton numbered fifty-nine and the number of lots built upon had increased by sixteen to a total of fifty. The east side of Parsons had begun in the century's second decade to economically take-off, as sixty lots by 1920 had been surveyed, of which thirty-one contained a structure. By block, the comparison of total lots to lots built upon looks like this: [16]

West Side of Parsons, 1920	East Side of Parsons, 1920
Railroad to Hosack --------- 6 of 7 lots built upon	Railroad to Hosack ------- 0 of 11 lots
Hosack to Barthman ------- 16 of 16 lots built upon	Hosack to Marion -------- 4 of 9 lots
Barthman to Reeb --------- 7 of 11 lots built upon	Marion to Innis ---------- 23 of 23 lots
Reeb to Innis -------------- 8 of 11 lots built upon	Innis to Woodrow ------- 4 of 17 lots
Innis to Woodrow --------- 13 of 14 lots built upon	

The filling up of business lots indicated an advancing growth of commercial activity. Judging by the increase in retail during the 1920s, the decade was one in which Parsons Avenue reached its take-off period. The growth began slowly, held back by a brief national recession in 1921. In 1922, the Steelton area retail and other businesses, such as the bank and the hotel, both south of Marion, numbered just twenty-five. In this year, it is interesting to note that residences still exceeded the number of retail shops. For 1922, the residences numbered eighteen from Woodrow to Innis, thirty-two from Innis to Reed, forty-four from Reed to Barthman/Marion, and nineteen from Marion to the railroad tracks – a total of 113.[17] It may not have appeared that residences had such a numerical dominance, for it was common for individuals and families to live in a small house to the rear of a business establishment that fronted on Parsons. Many other residents lived on the second floor of a street level retail shop.

But prosperity brought a rapid increase in retail from the early 1920s to the end of the decade. Playing a significant role in this retail growth was the Schottentstein family, whose flagship store on Parsons Avenue soon became the dominant retail enterprise on the South Side.

Schottenstein Retailers

Among Parsons Avenue commerce, one retail store for decades dominated Steelton and Parsons Avenue shopping. Its official name as of 1934 was E.L. Schottenstein and Company, a department store at the northwest corner of Reeb and Parsons avenues. According to Morris Schottenstein's family history, the genesis of the department store dates to 1914 when Ephraim, Morris's uncle, opened an enterprise called the "Reliable Store." But first, we will outline other Schottenstein family retail on Parsons Avenue. Ephraim had three brothers, Meyer, Harry, and Abraham, all of whom opened retail stores of shorter duration than the department store. In 1915 Meyer and Harry opened "Schottenstein Brothers" on Parsons near Barthman Avenue. Selling only men's clothes, the brothers dealt in seconded merchandise and consignment goods from Cincinnati. Although this business, according to Morris's account, thrived, it appears to have closed about 1925, the year in which Harry opened a shoe store in the same block of Parsons. Two years later, Harry was operating a general merchandise store about a block north of the shoe store. This latest store selling goods for men, women, and children became large enough to need five salesmen. Although making "good money," Harry left the business at the end of 1928, a tenure of less than two years. In the late 1920s, Abraham opened the "Fair Store" at 1837 Parsons, just north of Innis Avenue and closed it in 1930. According to Morris's history, all these stores handled similar merchandise and "all did well."

Although the smaller Schottenstein stores lasted but a few years each, the flagship store growing from Ephraim's "Reliable Store" would serve South Side shoppers for about ninety years, becoming a Parsons Avenue institution. In Morris Schottenstein's words this store became "the primary liquidation and retail outlet in Central Ohio," growing to department store status as it expanded several times from the corner of Reeb Avenue. By 1945, the store had acquired four storefronts to its north, taking up most of the block. As he remembered the store as it was about 1940, Morris wrote:

> The E.L. Schottenstein and Company, as the business was known by 1934, was a spacious and inviting store. The merchandise, such as shirts, pants, underwear, and even hats was kept in glass cases or displayed on open shelves. Suits were hanging on the sides. The Ladies's Department was carpeted. It displayed, with a good deal of taste, such items as dresses, skirts, blouses, hose, and lingerie. Children's clothes, of all types, were found in the middle of the store. The shoes were housed in the second store, the original building which had been on the second lot from the corner. Presently, both stores were connected

in the interior. As one entered the stsore, one sensed that things were organized, and that the salespeople were on their toes.[18]

Schottenstein's and Company was an anchor on Parsons Avenue, drawing so many shoppers that neighboring retailers felt a positive impact. Since the Schottenstein family was Jewish, the department store was always closed on Saturday, the Jewish sabbath, and opened all day Sunday. So strong was the Schottenstein market strength that other retailers who would normally be open on a Saturday also closed and opened on Sunday, for the obvious reason that gentile retailers would have more customers on Schottenstein's work day.

Retail Growth After 1922

While Schottenstein's was expanding, the overall growth of Parsons Avenue commercialism was impressive, as the number of business establishments reached eighty-five by 1929, more than a three-fold increase in seven years. The block by block comparison of commercial outlets in the two years shows the following.

Commercial Outlets, Parsons Avenue		
	1922	1929
Woodrow to Innis -------------	2	10
Innis to Reeb --------------------	6	14
Reeb to Barthman /Marion ---	7	31
Barthman/Marion to Kian ----	12	16
Hosack to railroad tracks ------	0	14
	___	___
	27	85

There were still in 1929 a significant number of residences on Parsons Avenue, even as storefronts were replacing private homes. Morris Schottenstein in the following quotation from his family history refers to the presence of private homes on Parsons. It is also a statement of the diversity and vitality of Parsons Avenue in the early 1930s:

South Parsons Avenue, in the Steelton area, was a region where foreigners settled and did business. One found there such enterprises as the Foreign Grocery where one could buy tickets and send them to their loved ones to join them in America. The Foreign Grocery also held money for its patrons. The Steelton District was composed of both homes and commercial establishments. The main artery, Parsons Avenue, was lined by stores, offices, and homes. As one looked south from Woodrow Avenue, one saw a wide street with a streetcar traveling down the center. The rails were imbedded in the brick. The businesses or offices were usually two-storied. In most cases, the offices were located on the second floor. The typical commercial building was of wood with show windows and a center or side entrance exposing a stairway. Homes were interspersed along the avenue. The homes were usually doubles with large porches. It was not unusual to see people Parsons sitting on their porches while others walked the streets, seeking goods. Life along South Avenue was very brisk. People shopped enthusiastically (when the business cycle was good). The streets were clean and orderly. One found a great variety of business establishments.

The authors of "South Side: A History" also called attention to the vitality of Steelton, writing of the 1920s into the 1940s, they stated: "The most important commercial center grew in the heart of Steelton itself. Beginning at the Parsons Avenue viaduct (location of Buckeye Steel) and continuing for several blocks, this vibrant collection of stores and restaurants, professional offices, theatres and bars became a second downtown for South Siders."[19]

Over the years of Parsons Avenue's busy life, the electric streetcar complemented the street's vitality. In 1893, the Columbus and Central Railway was granted a city franchise to operate an electric streetcar along Parsons from Livingston Avenue to the corporation line at the railroad tracks. Shortly after the Parsons streetcar began operations, the tracks of the older line along Mohawk Street (in today's German Village) were extended southward along Fourth Street to Barthman Avenue in Steelton, then along Barthman east to Parsons where it connected with the Parsons line.[20]

Foreign Grocery: Many Steelton businesses developed a uniqueness, accentuating the attractiveness of Parsons Avenue. The Foreign Grocery was one of these. This enterprise was opened about 1910 by William Trautman and Alex Gaal on the east side of Parsons near Barthman Avenue. Most of the customers in the early years were first generation immigrants who did not speak English, a situation met by the employment of multi-lingual clerks. The store not only stocked food from the old countries, but became an emporium selling clothing, shoes, hardware, and miscellaneous items. In addition to the retail, the grocery was the conduit for customers wishing to send money to relatives in Europe. Moreover, the store became the agent for the Cunard Ship Line, selling tickets to Europe. Other services included extending credit to worthy customers and even granting loans. Dispatch writer Betty Daft in 1979 interviewed John Gaal, grandson of the original owner, Alex Gaal, who told her that he "delivered groceries all over the South Side, and knew them (customers) all. There was at least 100 families of Hungarians and nearly that many Croatians and Serbs."[21]

In 1925, the grocery moved across Parsons and just south of Marion Road to 1957-59 Parsons Avenue, where it remained until 1958, closing in that year, a victim of the chain super markets.

In the second decade of the century, Steelton was deemed worthy of a bank, an institution that never saw the light of day in Flytown or Milo-Grogan. A large downtown bank, the

Commonwealth Citizens Trust and Savings, in 1917 opened a branch bank on the east side of Parsons Avenue, just south Marion Road, very near the Foreign Grocery. The branch served Steelton at this address until 1928, when it moved to 1873 Parsons, just south of Reeb Avenue. In the early 1930s, while still at the same location, it became the Ohio National Bank, surviving there into the 1980s.

Motion picture theatres added to Parsons Avenue's vitality. During the 1920s, the Innis Theatre, located just north of Innis Avenue was a well-attended venue. Later it became the Russell Theatre. During the same decade, Steelton residents also supported the Wonder Theatre, showing popular movies just south of Barthman Avenue on Parsons.

Maturity & Decline

In the early 1930s, when Columbus's industrial output decreased by over $70 million, the number of retail outlets over many areas of the city held their own. We saw in Part II that this was the case in Milo-Grogan. In Steelton, the pattern was the same. With its well populated housing area, Steelton and other South Side residents supported the Parsons Avenue shops to the extent that the number of commercial storefronts actually increased from eighty-five in 1929 to eighty-nine in 1940. A block by block comparison before and just after the depression shows:

	1929 Parsons Ave. Businesses	1940 Parsons Ave Business
Woodrow to Innis	10	19
Innis to Reeb	14	21
Reeb to Barthman/Marion	31	23
Barthman/Marion to Kian	16	20
Kian to Hosack	5	3
Hosack to railroad tracks	9	3
	----	----
	85	89

At this point in Parsons Avenue history, the surge in retail growth that began in the mid 1920s had reached its maturity, and the business establishments leveled out for about two decades before the factory decline began to take its toll. As Morris Schottenstein put it: "By 1940 South Parsons Avenue had taken the form that it would have until the era of the sixties, when it would see a decline."[22]

Although Parsons Avenue remained full of shoppers well into the 1960s, by 1969 a dip in retail support had occurred, and the number of commercial shops had fallen to seventy-six from the 1940 high of eighty-nine. Over the next decade, the dip had turned into a near flood, as shoppers for the first time failed to adequately support Parsons Avenue retail, and by 1980, commercial outlets had plunged to forty-three. Along with the closing retail came the dreaded vacancies that had given Milo-Grogan such a decayed appearance. In 1969, there were over thirty in the Steelton area of Parsons. As residents shopped into the 1970s, they increasingly saw littered doorways, broken glass, and plywood nailed over doors and windows of former retail shops, as if the neighborhood was advertising a cancerous condition. The declining retail by block showed: [23]

	1969 Parsons Ave Businesses	1980 Parsons Ave Businesses
Woodrow to Innis	14	10
Innis to Reeb	23	12
Reeb to Barthman/Marion	14	6
Barthman/Marion to Kian	14	10
Kian to Hosack	8	4
Hosack to railroad tracks	3	1
	----	----
	76	43

Factory Decline

Fundamental to the decline of Parsons Avenue retail was the crash of Steelton's industrial plant. Columbus's industrial communities were always a two-edged sword. The humming of the factories resulted in a growing community with lively retail and a stable neighborhood buttressed by institutional support. But neighborhood deterioration, in the absence of intervening action, inevitably followed factory closings, with social as economic repercussions. (See Harrington's comment at end of Part II.)

The reasons for the loss of industry are many: (1) loss of market – the case of Buckeye Steel; (2) purchase by outside corporation with no local interest – the case of Seagrave, Federal Glass, and Hercules; (3) foreign competition – the case also of Federal Glass; (4) environmental regulations – the situation of Case Manufacturing; and (5) physical location no longer satisfactory – all of Steelton and Milo-Grogan.

Taking a long backward view, the 1920s was probably a watershed decade in Steelton history, for even in that early decade, the industrial cluster may have already been behind the historical curve. This was the conclusion of the authors of "South Side: A History." They wrote: "The South Side reached its full industrial potential during the 1920s. The next four decades saw little in the way of economic development. Instead, an increasingly aging set of factories tried to adapt themselves to a changing national marketplace."[24] This struggle to adapt can be at least partly seen in a brief consideration of the decline and/or closing of major Steelton factories.

<u>Seagrave Corporation:</u> In an ironic turn for many factories, Seagrave in 1963 sold its truck and fire equipment division because its current facilities in Steelton were inadequate to meet the demand for its fire products. Long before the sale, however, Seagrave had become a different company, having in the 1950s diversified into paint and industrial finishes, leather tanning, low cost homes, and biochemical refuse deposal. The sale made Seagrave a division of FWD Corporation of Pennsylvania. With the $2.7 sale price, the officers of Seagrave hoped to expand its product base even more, though it would no longer be independent. But the parent corporation felt the ancient plant along South High Street was far too small to handle the product line, and in 1965 moved the entire operation to Clintonville, Wisconsin, leaving about 300 Seagrave workers unemployed. Seagrave had been in Steelton since 1898.

<u>Chase Foundry and Manufacturing Company:</u> By the early 1980s, Chase Foundry was down to about twenty workers in the foundry and ten in the materials section from a high of 100 in the 1940s and forty-five in 1953. In January 1984, the twenty foundry workers lost their jobs when the Ohio Environmental Protection Agency mandated the foundry's closing due to the company's failure to install pollution control equipment. Chase had repeatedly refused to install the controls, citing excessive cost.[25] Chase Foundry had been in Steelton since 1896.

<u>Buckeye Steel Castings Company:</u> Buckeye was a company that seemed to be perennially struggling to adjust to changing market trends. The trend it could not shed was the decline of the country's railroads, its only customer for its primary product, the railroad car coupler. According to Blackford's company history, Buckeye's outlook became dire in 1958 when it lost money, and for the next five years, had a negative net income or was barely above the line. Its bleak outlook forced the company to take serious steps to diversify. In the early 1960s, Buckeye for the first time secured both a Chairman of the Board and a President from outside the company. Fresh thinking soon led Buckeye to invest in products unrelated to railroad couplers. By the late 1960s, the company had acquired two Ohio based plastics companies that manufactured plastic parts for automobiles and in 1969, these acquisitions accounted for thirty-seven percent of Buckeye's sales. This success led to the purchase of four more companies between 1972 and 1976, three of which boosted Buckeye's bottom line. By 1977, steel castings made up just forty percent of company sales. While diversification was succeeding, Buckeye invested over fifteen million dollars for internal improvements that included two new electric furnaces that replaced the open hearth types, the second coming in the mid 1970s at a cost of $2.6 million. These investments reduced the cost of steel production from $62 to $55 million per ton.

In the 1970s while showing increasing sales, Buckeye itself became a take-over target, the most serious one coming from Dayton-Walther of Dayton, Ohio. In the meantime,

Worthington Industries of Worthington, Ohio had been purchasing Buckeye stock. Since Buckeye's management collectively owned just five percent of company shares, the officers did not feel that they could repel Worthington, and opened negotiations for sale of the company. In 1980 Buckeye Steel became a wholly owned subsidiary of Worthington Industries, an arrangement that lasted until 1999, when Worthington sold Buckeye to Key Equity Capital. Once again Buckeye was an independent corporation and still located at its 1902 Steelton site. But independence failed to translate into prosperity, as an industry wide downturn, accentuated by the November 2001 terrorist attack, forced Buckeye to file for bankruptcy and cease all operations in October 2002, putting some 700 employees out of work.

But after being closed for only five months, a group of investors, some from Worthington Industries, purchased Buckeye out of bankruptcy for about $15 million. Re-opening in March 2003, the former Buckeye Steel was now the Columbus Steel Castings Company with the former president of Worthington Industries, Donald Malenick, as the chief executive. After six years, the new company continues to operate without a union, worker pay being based on a performance formula geared to employee contribution to company profit. As of 2009, Columbus Steel employed just under 1,000 workers.

While Columbus Steel was attempting to climb out of its debt sinkhole, the company is having its problems with the Ohio Environmental Protection Agency (EPA). In June 2008, the EPA took Columbus Steel to court over excessive smoke and dust emanating from the Parsons Avenue plant, and was ordered to adopt a plan to reduce air pollution. Yet six months later, the company had failed to comply with the court order.

In addition to Columbus Steel's air quality problems, the U.S. Department of Labor's Occupational Safety and Health Administration (OSHA) cited the company in 2006 for over sixty violations of OSHA rules concerning worker exposure to silica, a substance harmful to human lungs. These violations resulted in fines totaling over $250,000. Moreover, in 2007 and 2008, OSHA cited Columbus Steel for exposing workers to welding rays, which resulted in proposed fines of $102,000.[26]

Federal Glass: Among the Marion Road factories, the closing of Federal Glass was the heaviest blow to Steelton, the blow appearing even heavier because of the suddenness of the closing. After the end of the first shift on January 31, 1979, the scheduled second shift found the doors locked – permanently. Although not aware of a closing date, Federal Glass workers had felt an uneasiness for the past two years. For in 1977, Federal Glass's parent company announced that it would sell Federal Glass to Lancaster Colony Corporation of Columbus for $4.5 million. Then, according to Federal Glass's plant manager, Jack Spengler, power politics entered the picture. The two giants of the glass industry, Anchor Hocking of Lancaster and Libby Glass, a division of Owens-Illinois of Toledo, may not have wanted the sale to be made, for if concluded Colony Glass with the assets of Federal Glass would be in a strong position from which to compete equally with the two industry leaders. The giants then, surmised Spengler, pressured the Federal Trade Commission (FTC) to block the sale. Using the anti-trust law, FTC forbade the sale, maintaining the Federal Glass was financial sound. (Generally, mergers and sales are prohibited if both companies are strong, but are allowed if one company is financially weak and on the verge of closing.)

Federal Glass's plant manager disputed the FTC conclusion that Federal Glass was financially sound, a position supported by the president of the glass workers' union after the union's accountant examined the company's financial records and concluded in 1978 that there was not much hope of Federal Glass's survival. After the FTC ruled against the proposed sale, the union president appealed for a thirty-day stay in order to present arguments for keeping the plant open. After the FTC denied the stay, the last hope for a sale was lost, and Federal Glass made its sudden closing, resulting in a loss of 1,500 jobs. Federal Glass had been in Steelton since 1904.

Federal Glass plant in 1919.

Bonney-Floyd Company: In early 1964, Bonney-Floyd was purchased by the Shenango Furnace Company of Pittsburgh, but the factory would continue to operate at its Steelton site, as a division of Shenango. At the time of the sale, Bonney-Floyd's employment was about 350, down from 525 in 1953. Putting a good face on the sale, Bonney-Floyd's president, John Bonney, announced that the company hoped for a rebound in sales and employment. But the new match was apparently a poor one, as financial losses and labor problems resulted in Shenango permanently closing the Steelton plant in February 1972, with a loss of 375 jobs. Bonney-Floyd had been in Steelton since 1904.

Hercules Box Company: Hercules once a leading national company in corrugated box manufacturing was purchased in the early 1970s and became Columbus Container, a division of Continental Corregated Corporation, which closed the Marion Road plant in the early 1980s. In the early 1960s, Hercules had employed about 300 workers. Hercules had been in Steelton since 1911.

<u>Lattimer-Stevens Company:</u> Lattimer-Stevens survived until the mid 1980s, closing on its own. At the time, the company was producing gas fittings for utility companies. At closing Lattimer had employed 115 workers. Lattimer had been in Steelton since the mid 1930s.

Some Steelton companies had closed earlier than the above named plants. One of the earliest to depart was the J.W. Brown Manufacturing Company, the early maker of carriage lamps and then automobile lights. It did not survive the depression decade of the 1930s. Brown had been in Columbus since 1899 and in Steelton since 1913. One of the oldest of the Steelton factories, having located on Marion Road in 1895 was the Brightman Manufacturing Company. After sixty years in Steelton, it closed in the mid 1950s, putting about sixty men out of work. The American Blower Company, opening in 1938 on Marion Road, appeared to be successful and was moderately large, employing about 470 workers in the early 1950s but in the mid 1960s it was sold and became the American Standard Industrial Company, which left Columbus in 1969. One of the smallest of Steelton players in terms of employment was the Linde Air Products Company, which opened on Marion Road in the 1930s. It closed in the early 1990s.[27]

While most Steelton factories were closing or declining, two Marion Road factories bucked the downward trend. Brown Steel, which located in Steelton in the late 1920, and was later purchased by Lapham-Hickey Steel. To date Brown appears to be doing well under the new owner, producing automated machines and contracting for precision metal slitting. As of 2008, Brown had ten to twenty million dollars in revenue. But Brown's success could not reverse the decline of Steelton, as the capital intensive company employed just twenty to fifty skilled workers.

Buckeye Stamping, a 1910 Marion Road company, turned itself away from stamping glassware (an endeavor with little future since American glassware was declining) to producing electronic enclosures, as film containers and canisters. In addition, the company found a niche in the manufacturing of precision instrument knobs, air tank liners, and card ejectors. The markets it serves are associated with aerospace, the military, and telecommunications. One of Buckeye's divisions is called Buckeye Shapeform, which supplies Lockheed Martin with specific technology for tactical missiles. Annual sales as of 2008 are in the nine million-dollar range. But like Brown Steel, Buckeye Stamping's high tech workforce is only about sixty, hardly anything that would give Steelton a boost.[28]

Steelton Turned on Its Head

In November 1983, the Columbus Dispatch headlined an article: "Job losses cripple South Side." The writer added that during the past five years, the South Side had lost 3,000 factory jobs, resulting in an unemployment rate of thirty percent,[29] according to the president of the South Side Business Association. Throughout the 1980s and 1990s, the South Side economy continued its downward slide. Many residents moved out. The poor with little job skills who could afford only cheap housing moved into abandoned houses. These newcomers had no stake nor felt any pride toward the neighborhood and as a result Steelton housing took a nosedive.

In the 1930s when Morris Schottenstein wrote of houses on Barthman and Reeb avenues as "well painted with a groomed yard" and "no signs of urban decay," such houses by the 1990s could be counted on one hand. Instead, Barthman and Reeb houses had become vacant and many vandalized. Others faced the street with boarded windows and doors, in an attempt to keep out vandals. Occupied houses had become characterized by littered and unkempt front yards, some with cars parked in the yard. Adding to the deterioration, cracked and broken sidewalks went unrepaired. The city government appeared to have no interest in the neighborhood, as curbs and streets were left with potholes and strewn with debris. On Fourth Street near Innis, a large frame house sits empty, partially burned, a victim of arson.

The advent of the poor and transient residents without stable jobs was followed by increasing crime in the neighborhood. A Barthman Avenue resident and president of the Southside Neighbors Against Crime told the Dispatch in March 2005 that she could see drug dealers, prostitutes, and car thieves from her front window.[30]

However, Woodrow Avenue at the northern end of Steelton has escaped the gross deterioration that characterizes Barthman and Reeb, as the mostly single family homes have to date been well maintained. To the street's benefit, Woodrow appears to be the nexus of the Hungarian Village, an organization formed in the mid 1970s under the leadership of the pastor of the Hungarian United Church of Christ, now the Hungarian Reformed Church. As mentioned earlier, this church, about a block west of Parsons, remains in a good state of repair and supported by a caring congregation. The other Hungarian Church, the Catholic St Ladislas Church for Hungarians adds a note of care and optimism on Barthman Avenue. It too is well maintained along with the 1916 parish school, which continues to educate the churches' children.

Contemporary photo of the Hungarian Reformed Church on Woodrow Avenue.

Another Steelton light that continues to burn is the South Side Settlement House that began about 1910 on Reeb Avenue, and was supported in its early years by Buckeye Steel. The settlement house remained at the Reeb location until the late 1970s, when it moved to larger and improved quarters on Innis Avenue where it continues its mission of improving the lives of South Siders.

<u>Parsons Avenue:</u> Parsons Avenue by the 1980s in Steelton was a shadow of its former self. We noted above that the retail shops during the 1970s had been reduced by one-half. Some of the closed stores were replaced with other businesses, but the new retail did not measure up to the quality of those of earlier decades. Two prominent stores that had closed not to be replaced by similar quality were the Fountain Drug Store and the Steelton Market. The Fountain Drug had been a retail landmark since it opened in 1913 at Parsons and Innis Avenue. It thrived for decades before closing in August 1991, a victim of weak sales brought on by the factory closings and lack of worker paychecks.

The Steelton Market, without the long pedigree of many Steelton stores, soon became a popular shopping destination. It opened in 1963 at Parsons and Reeb, near Schottenstein's and was operated by the original owner until September 2001, who at that time planned to retire and close the store. But Bill Shook thought the financial statements looked good, took a chance, and bought the grocery. Unfortunately, his timing was bad. Many of the store's customers were Buckeye Steel families, and when the plant closed about a year later with a loss of 700 jobs, grocery sales sank. Although Buckeye reopened under new ownership later, it was too late and too little for Shook. From $2.4 million in sales the first year, sales fell to $1.4 million the second year. In the spring of 2003, the market closed.[31] Also closing in the 1970s and 1980s were such retail mainstays as Dots Jewelry Store, Longs Drug Store, Bush Hardware, and the Steelton Furniture Store (a Schottenstein enterprise).

Instead of retail like these, Steelton by the 1970s saw its share of short-lived used furniture stores, junk shops, and thrift stores selling cheap used clothing and household goods. These were stores whose customers were the poor and the transient, not the middle-class stable factory workers of past years. Such shoppers were now few and far between. Without the middle-class, the Ohio National Bank, which under a former name, had been in Steelton since 1917 and at its current location at Parsons and Reeb since 1928, could no longer increase its capital base and closed in 1989.

Reflecting the deteriorating and criminal quality of the neighborhood, Schottenstein's Department Store in the mid 1980s was forced to board its glass front doors and windows facing Parsons Avenue as a protection against break-ins. With sales declining in the troubled area, Schottenstein's lost its commitment to maintain an attractive and inviting store for shopping; paint remained chipped, fixtures were not repaired, and when the large "S" from its sign fell in 2004, it was not put back. The inevitable came in February 2005 when the Parsons Avenue institution closed permanently. Its peak employment had been in excess of 100, but at closing it was far under the peak.[32]

The 1945 photo at top shows a lively and diversified Parsons Avenue. The 2010 photo at bottom shows the same section of Parsons. The movie theatre was at the location of the fence, and to the right of the two-story building, all structures have been demolished, as the retail is half or less than it was in 1945.

PostScript

Well before the Schottenstein closing when the factories were taking their last breath and Parsons Avenue retail seem to be in a free fall, the city government proposed a plan in the early 1970s that would have razed the Steelton neighborhood so that an industrial park could be constructed. (Were they still impressed with the destruction of Flytown some fifteen years earlier?) Residents formed the Reeb-Hosack Planning Committee and fought off the proposed razing of their homes. The Committee moved on to secure grants and loans from the city and federal government for street, sidewalk, and lighting improvement. But before much of an impression had been made, the recession of the late 1970s and early 1980s brought the funds to an end.

Some individuals attempted to promote Steelton to private industry. Where Federal Glass had been located, the Federal Industrial Park was established, but it was a struggle and new businesses were hard to procure. In a troubled community, private enterprise sees too much risk and largely avoids the area, leaving public investment as the only avenue to improvement.

After the Schottenstein closing, the city administration of Mayor Michael Coleman indicated some interest in leading a Steelton revitalization attempt. A spokesman for the Mayor put on a brave face, stating that the Schottenstein closing has ... "opening up a new realm of possibility." The city has in recent years shown an interest in leading redevelopment efforts of deteriorating areas of Columbus by injecting large sums of money into, for example, the Northland Mall area, the downtown Lazarus building, and the Sullivant Gardens housing project in Franklinton. Currently the city is spearheading the razing of the failed City Center Mall and the planned construction of an urban park.

In Steelton, the city administration has in recent years demolished the Schottenstein Department Store and the nearby Steelton Market, but since 2008 the city budget has not supported a large scale investment project. And so the "new realm of possibility" has yet to see daylight.[33]

Columbus and Manufacturing

With the demise of the industrial communities of the Olentangy, Milo-Grogan, and Steelton, Columbus has seen the last of such integrated neighborhoods. These communities developed because in the early 20th century, Columbus was a walking city with an efficient railroad network. The passing of time has erased both. The combination of zoning, four and six lane innerbelts and outerbelts, mass production of automobiles and trucks, and environment regulations have sent factories to the edge of cities.

As the industrial communities were fading into history in the later half of the 20th century, Columbus was becoming less of a manufacturing city. The industrial workforce was increasingly not holding to its historical twenty-five percent of the city's total employment. In 1960, the Columbus area manufacturing employment comprised thirty percent of the total workforce. (These figures are from the census bureau's Metropolitan Statistical Area or MSA, an area larger than Columbus's political boundary.) By 2000, Columbus's MSA manufacturing workforce had declined to eleven percent of the total, as the city's service sector began to dominate the workforce. In this period, employment is such areas as wholesale and retail trade, finance, banking, transportation, government, and insurance increased in absolute terms from 283,000 in 1970 to 730,000 in 2000.

Another way of looking at Columbus's declining manufacturing is by considering the city's twenty-five largest employers. In 1981, only Timken Ball Bearing of Milo-Grogan made the list, and it was number twenty-five with 1,850 workers, a figure that pales in relation to the top three employers – the State of Ohio with 28,300 employees, Ohio State University with 17,700, and the federal government with 11,100. Five other manufacturers made the list, two being "new type" factories on the city's outskirts. One was General Motors, which opened on the far west side in 1946 and the other was Western Electric, opening in 1959 on the far east side. By 1999, none of the 1981 manufacturing companies made the top twenty-five, though two other manufacturers had been added, one being Honda placing fourth with 13,000 employees and the other being Lucent Technologies with 3,890 workers. Honda is something of a stretch, since it is located in the independent city of Marysville, which is about twenty miles northwest of Columbus, but it falls within the MSA. The top three employers remained the same as in 1981.[34]

Endnotes

Prelude and Part 1

1. Alfred Lee. History of the City of Columbus, Munsell Co. New York, 1992, Vol. I, p.201.
2. William Martin. History of Franklin County, Follett, Foster and Co., Columbus, 1858, p.296.
3. Roderick D. McKenzie. "The Neighborhood: A Study in the Local Life in the City of Columbus, Ohio." The American Journal of Sociology, Vol 27, Sept 1921, p. 151.
4. Henry L. Hunker. Industrial Evolution of Columbus, Ohio. Bureau of Business Research, Ohio State University, 1958, chapters 5-8.
5. For the changing Columbus downtown, see two books in the Images of America series: Richard Barrett. Columbus 1860-1910. Arcadia Press, 2005. Also by Barrett, Columbus 1910-1970. See Also Robert Samuelson. Architecture: Columbus. Published by Columbus Chapter AIA, 1976.
6. Edward H. Miller. The Hocking Valley Railway. Ohio University Press, 2007,pp 20-23.
7. Henry Failing. First Report of the Business and Prospects of the City of Columbus. Ohio State Journal Printing House, 1873, p.5 Quoted in Hunker, ibid., p.45.
8. Quoted in Hunker, ibid, p.46.
9. Osman C. Hooper. History of the City of Columbus, Ohio, 1797-1920.Memorial Publishing Co. Columbus, 1920, p. 221.
10. McKenzie, ibid. p. 146
11. Hunker, ibid. chapters 3,4,5. Also Columbus city directories for appropriate years.
12. Architecture: Columbus, AIA Chapter, ibid. p.120.
13. Architecture: Columbus, AIA Chapter, ibid., p.106.
14. Charles C. Winter. A Concise History of Columbus, Ohio and Franklin County. Xlibis, 2009, p.84.
15. Columbus Citizen Journal, 2-24-1968. Also see Hunker, ibid. chapters 4 and 5.
16. McKenzie, ibid. p.155.
17. Helton, Francesca Colonna. Flytown and the Italian Community, 1858-1930. Self-published, 1970.
18. Jon A. Peterson. "From Settlement of Social Aging: Settlement Work in Columbus, Ohio, 1898-1958." Social Science Review, Vol 39, No 2, 1965, pp.191-208. Quote on p.191. On Flytown generally see Betty Garrett. Columbus: America's Crossroads. Continental

Heritage Press, 1980, pp 86-87 and p.119. Also Columbus Dispatch 8-9-1992 and Citizen-Journal, Ben Hayes, 1-1-1974 and 5-5-1975.

19. Peterson. "From Social Settlement..." ibid, 191-205.

20. McKenzie. Ibid, pp 353 and 152-153.

21. Brian Higgins. Village Vibe, May 2000.

22. Hunker. Ibid, p. 109. Also Columbus City Directory for 1937.

23. Garrett. Columbus... Ibid, p.119. Columbus Call and Post 2-18-1999. Also Peterson. "From Social Settlement ... ibid, p. 204.

24. Columbus City Plan, 1957, p.53, plate 19. Also Betty Daft, Columbus Dispatch 1-20-1980. Quote isbuy Ed Lentz. This Week, 11-1-1993.

25. Robert W. Adams. Urban Renewal Politics: A Case Study of Columbus, Ohio 1952-1961. Ph.D Dissertation, OSU 1970, pp,122-133 and 184-190 and 283. Also Columbus Citizen 1-6-1952; Columbus Dispatch 1-23-1952 and 8-28-1956. Ohio State Journal 1-24-1952. Also Columbus City Bulletin, Dept of Public Safety, Annual Report 1960.

26. Quote from Village Vibe 7-13-2000. Dairy Company information from Columbus Dispatch 9-18-1983.

27. The Arena District: A Neighborhood 170 Years in the Making. Nationwide Realty Investors, Columbus 2006.

Part 11

1. Italian Villge Newsletter, February 1997. Ohio Public Power Educational Institute newsletter, Winter 1997. Neighborhood News Control, 10-19-1998.

2. This discussion of Jeffrey company was taken from a pamphlet entitled "A Short History of the Jeffrey Company" by Robert H. Jeffrey II, who is the great-grandson of the founder and a former company President. It was written in April 1975. Also see Columbus Citizen 5-25-1949. Columbus Dispatch 12-12-1967, 1-2-1966 and 5-22-1977.

3. For annexation background see: Columbus Dispatch 2-27-1989 and 2-10-1910. For meeting quotes 2-3-1907 Columbus Citizen 10-16-1908. Ohio State Journal 10-14-1908. For annexation date and statistics see Report of the Chief Engineer in Columbus Annual Report of 1910, p.389.

4. Columbus Board of Trade Bulletin, July 1902. Also Columbus Dispatch 10-2-1977 and 6-2-1990. Hunker. Ibid, p, 97. Also Columbus city directories.

5. Miami Valley Historical Society newsletter January 1983. Columbus Citizen 2-3-1920. Columbus Dispatch 12-10-1986, 4-27-2001 and 7-12-1992. Also Hunker, ibid, p.56

6. Larry Saylor." Street Railroads in Columbus, Ohio 1862-1920," The Old Northwest, Vol#3, Sept 1975.

7. Columbus city directories for appropriate years. Also employment statistics for early 1930s,

see Mansel Blackford. A Portrait Cast in Steel, Buckeye International and Columbus, 1881-1980. Greenwood Press, 1982,Westport, CT

8. United States Census, Characteristics of the Population, Report of the States for all appropriate Years.

9. City directories. Also Columbus Dispatch 8-5-1979, 7-12-1981 and 11-11-1996

10. Milo-Grogan Area Plan 1973, Planning Division, Dept of Development, City of Columbus (# 35) of The Columbus Plan 1970-1990.

11. Columbus Citizen 6-7-1967. Citizen Journal 5-9-1970. Also Moore, History of Columbus, ibid, 211-12.

12. Jeffrey. "A Short History ….", ibid, pp.33-35.

13. Columbus Dispatch 7-17-1993, 5-11-1995 and 9-24-1991. Business First 10-12-1992.

14. Milo-Grogan Neighborhood Plan, Planning Division, Dept of Development, City of Columbus, 2007.

15. Milo Arts brochure. Columbus Dispatch 4-6-2009.

16. Milo-Grogan Neighborhood Plan, 2007, ibid, p.62.

17. Columbus City Directory, 2007.

18. Michael Harrington. The Other America. McMillan, 1962, p.34

Part III

1. Hunker, ibid, p.48.

2. American Rolling Mill Company, The First Twenty Years, 1900=1922. Company printed, 1922. Also Hunker, ibid, p.54. Columbus Dispatch 7-3-1897. Unpublished paper on National Steel, located in Columbus Metro Library (business notebooks). Also city directories 1895-1920.

3. Matthew Lee. Seagrave : A Pictural History. Kalamazoo, MI 1991. Also Ohio State Journal 7-20-1930. Hunker, ibid, pp152 and 97. Columbus Didpatch 1-2-1932 and 8-31-1947.

4. Most of following summary taken from Mansel G, Blackford, A Portrait Cast in Steel: Buckeye International and Columbus, Ohio 1881-1980, Greenwood Press, 1982,pp. 23-37 and 94. Also Ohio State Journal 21-31-1952. Columbus Board of Trade Bulletin Oct 1902. Also Columbus Citizen 11-18-1908.

5 Unpublished paper c. 1960 in Columbus Metro Library (business notebook). Columbus Dispatch 9-13-1964. Hunker. Ibid. Columbus Dept of Development Notes, Dec 1986.

6. Osman C. Hooper. History of the City of Columbus, Ibid, p. 212 continuing. Hunker, ibid pp 54-57, 97 99. Columbus Dispatch 12-31-1954, 1-2-1964, and 9-13-1964. City directories

7. Morris Schottenstein. The Schottensteins, A Family Biographical Essay, Vol I, 1908-1930

and Vol II, 1930-1960. Orion Publications, Columbus 1987. Ref is to VolI, p. 9. Also Betty Daft, Columbus Dispatch 8-26-1979.

8. South Side: A History. Columbus Neighborhood Design Assistance Center, Columbus 1987. P.16. Also Baist's Real Estate maps for Columbus 1899, 1910, 1920. Also city directories.

9. Columbus City directories.

10. The Columbus Plan: 1970-1990. Columbus Dept of Development, Near East Side Area Plan # 33, Dec 1972. P. 1-10.

11. Schottenstein, ibid, Vol. II, p.28.

12. McKenzie, ibid, p.152. Daft, Columbus Dispatch 8-29-1979.

13. Hooper, ibid, pp 212-13. Also South Side: A History, ibid, p17.

14. Columbus Dispatch 8-26-1979. Also city directories.

15. Blackford, ibid, pp. 132-37.

16. Blaist's Columbus Real Estate maps for 1899, 1910, and 1920.

17. Columbus city directories.

18. Schottenstein, ibid, Vol. I, 164-165 an Vol.II, pp. 12 and 23.

19. Schottenstein, ibid, quote from Vol.II, p. 10. South Side: A History, ibid, quote, p.12.

20. South Side: A History, ibid, pp, 9-11.

21. Daft, Columbus Dispatch 8-29-1979.

22. Schottenstein, ibid, Vol II, p.23.

23. Columbus City directories.

24. South Side, ibid, p.19.

25. For Seagrave closing, see Columbus Business 1-29-1966 and Dispatch 12-8-1991. For Chase closing See Dispatch 1-27-1984.

26. Blackford, ibid.pp 148-163 and 193-203. Also Columbus Steel web site.

27. Bonney-Floyd, Dispatch 1-2-64 and 2-29-1972. Lattimer-Stevens, Dispatch 4-16-1992. Federal Glass Dispatch 2-1-1979 and 2-23-1979. City directories to trace years of closings Also for overview of Steelton closings see Dispatch 3-7-2005.

28. Web sites for Brown Steel Buckeye Stamping.

29. Columbus Dispatch 11-13-1983.

30. Columbus Dispatch 3-7-2005

31. Fountain Drug closing see Dipatch 8-2-1991. Steelton Market clsoing see Dispatch 3-7-2003.

32. Columbus Dispatch 2-10-2005 and 3-7-2005

33. Columbus Dispatch 3-7-2005 and 10-30-2005.

34. Henry Hunker. A Personal Geography. OSU 2000., pp.56-59.